'*Shame On Me* offers alternative routes into black life and suggests that there's still space for ... reflections on the politics of race presented in tangential ways.'

TLS

'This remarkable meditation on beautiful, human bodies formed by the violence of slavery and by colonial shame resists categorisation, even as it shows up the ways in which categories of race and identity are no more than empty methods of social control. Reading this book I felt a profound sense of relief: that someone as wise as Tessa McWatt had the compassion and courage to write it ... It is deeply moving, urgent and important.'

Preti Taneja, author of *We That Are Young*

'Lyrical and haunting ... McWatt forcefully demonstrates how we all have a stake in dismantling the status quo and creating new paths towards true freedom ... *Shame On Me* is a tale of our time, yet also timeless.'

The Saturday Paper

'Interrogating our ideas of race through the lens of her own multi-racial identity, critically acclaimed novelist Tessa McWatt turns her eye on herself, her body and this world in a powerful new work of non-fiction.'

Layla Saad, author of *Me and White Supremacy*

'Stunningly beautiful ... Her flowing, lyrical first-person prose is as close to poetry as prose can be, deeply evocative and laden with imagery without weighing the narrative down ... Deeply compelling and strikingly original.'

The Irish Times

'A brave indictment, both passionate and reflective, of the category of race and the prison that identity can become.'
Lisa Appignanesi, author of *Mad, Bad, and Sad*

'There have been many books about race and identity in recent years, but none quite like this one. *Shame On Me* is part memoir, part essay, and partly a challenge to think beyond the current parameters of "identity" in our contemporary world … Perceptive, poignant and deeply profound … It is an essential intervention on behalf of those of us who wish to confront and overcome the resurgence of racism today.'
Anshuman Mondal, Professor of Modern Literature at UEA

'Executed with mellifluous scholarship and an eagle's eye for affecting detail.'
Brixton Review of Books

'Heartstopping and wise, exquisitely written, compellingly told, *Shame On Me* rises to a crescendo of such beauty and grace in its final chapter — a call to activism and resistance — that it left me breathless with the intensity of my own listening.'
Rebecca Stott, author of *In the Days of Rain*

'*Shame On Me* is one of the most moving and intellectually profound books of its kind … Courageously intimate and beautifully written, it is everything I admire in Tessa McWatt.'
David Chariandy, author of *I've Been Meaning to Tell You*

'A remarkable achievement, both for the brilliance of its ambition as well as the realisation of it. McWatt's heritage is wide-reaching and encompasses the bloodlines of both oppressed peoples as well as their oppressors. By taking parts of her body — eyes, ass, hair etc — and assessing their cultural significance and currency, she examines her life's experience through personal and global history, trying to make sense of her place in the world. Beautifully written, beguiling and audacious — a triumph.'

Henry Layte, The Book Hive

'Poignant, provocative, beautifully written, Tessa McWatt's new memoir *Shame On Me* is an important, original, and deeply thoughtful book. McWatt asks the toughest, most searching of questions about race and belonging and offers answers that surprise and challenge us. I loved it.'

Jill Dawson, author of *The Language of Birds*

'Powerful and provocative.'

Sunday Life

'Profoundly moving and deeply reflective.'

2020 OCM Bocas Prize jury

'Beautifully written and courageously told.'

2020 Hilary Weston Writers' Trust Prize for Nonfiction jury

A BOOK OF THE YEAR FOR *THE GLOBE* AND *MAIL*

SHAME ON ME

Tessa McWatt is the author of six novels, two books for young people, and one nonfiction book. Her work has been nominated for the Governor General's Award, the Toronto Book Awards and the OCM Bocas Prize. She is a winner of the Eccles British Library Award 2018. McWatt is Professor of Creative Writing at UEA.

Tessa McWatt

Shame on me

a memoir of race and belonging

SCRIBE

Melbourne • London

Scribe Publications
2 John St, Clerkenwell, London, WC1N 2ES, United Kingdom
18–20 Edward St, Brunswick, Victoria 3056, Australia

Published by Scribe in 2019
This edition published 2021

The author is grateful to the Eccles Centre at the British Library for its support with this publication.

Extracts from *The God of Small Things* by Arundhati Roy on p.171, pp.188–9, and p.189,
copyright © Arundhati Roy, 1997, reproduced with permission from David Godwin Associates.
Extracts from *For Colored Girls Who Have Considered Suicide / When the Rainbow Is Enuf*
by Ntozake Shange on p.113, p.145, and pp.148–9 reprinted by the permission of Russell
& Volkening as agents for the author. Copyright © 1975 by Ntozake Shange.
Excerpt from 'Afterimages' from *Chosen Poems* © 1982, 1997 by Audre Lorde on p.225,
quoted by kind permission of Abner Stein.
Excerpt of 'Anodyne' from *Pleasure Dome: New and Collected Poems* © 2001 by Yusef Komunyakaa
published by Wesleyan University Press and reprinted on p.224 with permission.
Excerpt from 'Howl' by Allen Ginsberg on p.196. Copyright © 1956, Allen Ginsberg,
used by permission of The Wylie Agency (UK) Limited.
Excerpt from 'The Knife of Dawn' by Martin Carter on p.224 from *University of Hunger: Collected Poems &
Selected Prose*, Ed. Gemma Robinson (Bloodaxe Books, 2006).
Ossuary X1 by Dionne Brand. Copyright © 2010, Dionne Brand, used by permission of The Wylie
Agency (UK) Limited.
From *Night Sky with Exit Wounds* by Ocean Vuong published by Jonathan Cape. Reproduced by
permission of The Random House Group Ltd. © 2017
Extracts from Glass and God by Anne Carson published by Jonathan Cape reprinted by permission of The
Random House Group Limited © 1998
Excerpt from "The Sea Is History" from SELECTED POEMS by Derek Walcott, edited by Edward
Baugh. Copyright © 2007 by Derek Walcott. Reprinted by Permission of Farrar, Straus and Giroux.

Every effort has been made to acknowledge and contact the copyright holders for permission to reproduce
material contained in this book. Any copyright holders who have been inadvertently omitted from the
acknowledgements and credits should contact the publisher so that omissions may be rectified in subsequent
editions.

Printed and bound in the UK by CPI Group (UK) Ltd, Croydon CR0 4YY

Scribe Publications is committed to the sustainable use of natural resources and the use of paper products
made responsibly from those resources.

9781913348229 (UK edition)
9781925849011 (Australian edition)
9781925693812 (e-book)

Catalogue records for this book are available from the National Library of Australia
and the British Library.

scribepublications.co.uk
scribepublications.com.au

For Cicely

You think your pain and your heartbreak are unprecedented in the history of the world, but then you read.

JAMES BALDWIN

HYPOTHESIS

———

A young Chinese woman, so young, nearly still a girl, runs through a field of sugar cane. Her cotton shift is torn, her hair wild, there is fear on her face. My grandmother. She is escaping something terrible. Her legs are scraped by sharp stalks; blood is dripping from her knee. I imagine her eyes are streaming with tears. She is running because in her countryside village in Demerara, British Guiana, she has just been raped by her uncle.

I imagine my Indian ancestor as a strong woman, perhaps originally from Oudh, modern Uttar Pradesh, who could squat easily, hunched over green, sword-like leaves sprouting from emerging stalks. She is exhausted, pulling weeds out of unfamiliar soil in British Guiana. Thin, fragile from the 112-day journey by ship, she is lucky to have survived on a daily ration of beef or pork, suet, a biscuit, a few raisins.

My Arawak ancestor is in a dug-out corial on the Burro-Burro River that runs through the Iwokrama Forest. She paddles past a giant otter sunning itself on a tree stump.

My Portuguese ancestor, perhaps from Madeira, arrives among the first free immigrants to the colony in 1835. In her small hessian sac, she has hidden twenty delicate squares of lace that she stitched while watching her father haul his fishing nets from the sea.

———

There is a rumour about my French ancestor, but she will never confirm for anyone in the colony that her father had a chalice and a silver ring with a hexagram pattern, the Star of David, hidden in his suitcase when he arrived from France.

———

My African great-great grandmother is lost amongst trees that don't know her name, don't speak her language. Trees that have erased her. She can't find the path that will take her to the clearing. She is getting weak. I reach out to take her by the hand.

My Scottish great-great-great grandmother takes her last breath in East Lothian, and the book she has been reading falls across her chest. She never knows about the brown women with their hands in the soil.

EXPERIMENT

'What are you?'

The ducklings liked the new island
so much that they decided to live there.
All day long they follow the swan boats
and eat peanuts.

Eight years old, I am sitting near the back of the room in the grade-three classroom of my suburban Toronto elementary school. My desk is close to the window, and I am easily distracted by the birds, one particular bird that preens itself on a branch, its feathers shuttering up and down. I am not paying much attention to what the teacher is saying. We've been reading a book out loud together and I haven't been asked to read. I feel off the hook, set free to dream. A few minutes into daydreaming, I feel a change of tone in the teacher's voice and the class goes quiet. I snap out of my reverie. There's a question in the air. I look around at my classmates, who are looking at each other in search of an answer.

'Anyone know what that word means?' the teacher says.

Oh, I think, I'd better pay attention because there's a new word and I will need to know it.

'Does anyone know what Negro means?'

13

Good question, I think. What does that mean? I continue to look around at my classmates to see if anyone is going to come up with the answer or even a guess. The teacher seems anxious; this word has weight. Kenneth Percy puts up his hand. The teacher invites him to speak.

'Yeah, Tessa,' he says, as he points towards me at the back of the room.

Everyone in the class turns to face me. I freeze, my mind goes blank and all that is going on in my body is a low fizz like a misfiring electric circuit.

As I now realise, my teacher tries to rescue me from something she herself sees as a slur, a word that is fine in a book but not in person. 'Oh, no, not Tessa,' she says, to comfort me and all who might worry about what is in their midst. The other kids continue to stare at me.

Doing her job as the class's moral compass, she thinks fast: 'No, Tessa's something else.'

The misfiring electric circuit spews shocks through my cheeks, my arms and my legs, which begin to shake.

'What are you, Tessa?'

What am I?

I have no idea what she's asking. I feel as if I've failed a major test. I should have been paying attention, I should know how to answer this.

'You know, people are certain things,' she says, still trying to help, but wounding me deeper and deeper with every second she allows the class's eyes to remain on me. 'Things like, say, Mexican ...' She waits, but I have nothing. 'Brazilian ... Filipino ...' she carries on, offering possibilities she sees in my face, but in that moment

I hear only words that describe all the things that everyone else in the room isn't.

She waits, the circuit hums and it becomes so unbearable that I fold my arms on the desk and put my head onto them. I go away, deep inside myself. I don't remember where I go or for how long, but when I look up again everyone in the class has gone to recess and the teacher is wiping the board. She doesn't try to speak to me as I get up from my desk and leave the room, heavier now, saddled with something corrosive.

There, with my head in my arms, I learned that I could disappear; I could become invisible. I wondered why the teacher had not asked anyone else in the class the question, why my best friend didn't have to answer it. I kept these questions and my invisibility to myself.

I understood, without being able to articulate it, that language had the power to change me completely with the utterance of one word. I had known what black was — our extended family and friends were an array of shades — and I had known where I was from, but that wasn't what I had been asked. *Negro* was a word like *species*, a scientific word that clever people knew, but I didn't. I began to pay attention to the power of words. In being asked what I was and realising I did not know, I set off to find out. I believe it was the moment I became a writer.

———

Images visit me now as the sun sinks below the north London rooftops in Kilburn, where I sit at my desk, thinking about shame. They come in flashes like newsreels from the past.

15

There is my Chinese grandmother, running from rape. She is running also because she comes from a family of people who have running away in their DNA. Born to Chinese parents who had arrived in British Guiana from Hong Kong towards the end of the nineteenth century, my grandmother's family had escaped the Sino-Japanese War, after a different uncle, a dentist, had been strapped to his own dentist's chair and shot in the head by a Japanese soldier.

When I imagine my grandmother as a young woman, she is running.

My mother gave me the story of her mother's rape when I was a teenager. 'Granny ran away from the countryside,' she said, and nearly whispered the rest. I assumed it was her way of warning me about the perils of being a woman, as she had warned me about so many perils as a child. But it was the running and not the rape that stayed with me. I wanted to run towards something that was mine, like most teenagers do, and I wanted to understand what to do with all the words in constant motion in my mind. My mother often let slip nuggets of family history that were at times uncomfortable, at other times mysterious and poetic, and at still other times so distant and unreachable that they could only become myth. She had no way of knowing that she was feeding a writer, and I had no way of knowing what truths she was avoiding or concocting.

Like most families, mine is steeped in the anecdotes of grand-parents and parents who recount their histories through the lens of desire, aspiration, loss and shame. We Caribbean families rely heavily on oral histories because we come from ruptured roots, transplantation and whispered heritages related to slavery and colonialism. There are no solid family trees on traceable lineages for substantial strands of my ancestry, so there's no knowing for sure where, when or why my ancestors fled or were forcibly taken, or how they arrived in what officially became British Guiana in 1831.

Of course there are the grandparents I knew, and many uncles and aunts, both blood-related and not, but I can only imagine those who went before them. I know from stories that my ancestry includes Scottish, English, French, Portuguese, Indian, Amerindian, African and Chinese forebears. And there are rumours of hidden bloodlines — that possible French Jew.

My Indian ancestor's journey from the subcontinent might be one of those documented in the log books of governors and plantation overseers as they procured indentured labour for the colony. There was a scarcity of women. Slavery had been abolished; she was precious goods, arriving on a boat that carried 244 Indians, 233 of whom were men, six of them children, and only four other women. I imagine she resisted it, but necessity won out, and she was forced to bed the overseer to secure the chance of early freedom from her indenture contract.

Other stories bear the weight of secrets, like smuggled Portuguese lace, and they must never be openly mentioned. But some are playful and dance with the tropical light.

My indigenous great-great grandmother was described to me by my mother as a 'buck' ('My daddy's family had buck in dem,' she would say), a word that obscures the proper names of peoples — Arawak, Warrau, Arecuna, Akawaio, Patamona, Wapishana. *Buck* in the way my mother said it meant a wild thing, a man with a spear, a woman free to roam the jungle. I imagine this woman content, alone in her corial. When I paddle a canoe on a lake in Ontario

— bounded only by the earth, sky and water, while wildlife plays and hunts in the shadows along the shore — I am like her.

The Scottish McWatt of my surname and the English Eyre of my mother's side are my links to Europe. I had once imagined that I was secretly related to the Jane of my favourite book. But names themselves are unreliable. McWatt or Eyre might have been names my ancestors took to anglicise or legitimise themselves in a former slave colony. Whispers and shadows: a longing to belong to the mainstream of a new place after the rupture from their places of origin.

It's my African ancestor — my great-great grandmother — on whom I focus my imagination. She is the gap in my family's storytelling that I need to fill, though I can't trace her precise roots in Africa. Hers is the story that has been buried deepest, most painfully ignored. Hers is the story that bears such deep shame that it has been erased. But the body is a site of memory. If race is made by erecting borders, my body is a crossing, a hybrid many times over. My black and white and brown and yellow and red body is stateless, is chaos. Her body is stolen territory.

I am the result of the movement of bodies on ships: as captains; as cargo; as indentured servants; as people full of hope for a chance of survival. I also come from people nearly annihilated by those who arrived. Guyana, formerly British Guiana, a territory won by the British from Dutch and French treaties of war in the early 1800s, is the only English-speaking country in mainland South America. It is culturally Caribbean but geographically continental. Its pulsing river arteries connect mountains, savannah, rain forests and coastal plains. It is a land of jaguars, tapirs, giant anteaters, otters, monkeys and capybara, and it has one of the highest levels of biodiversity in the world. It is a land fought over for its natural resources, and its colonial history is a story that relies on ships from Europe, Africa, India, and China, along with the dug-out corials of the indigenous people. The paddles, the sails, the winches, the shackles.

My ancestry centres on one crop: sugar. My history pulses with moments of miscegenation, a hybridity that eludes any box I am asked to tick on census papers or job applications.

I am a song of sugar.

It's March. The London winter has been harsh — snow storms, icy pavements — nearly like a Toronto winter, where this year the freeze did not let up, with ice storms right out of disaster movies. Here at my desk I'm appreciating how much brighter it is at this time in the evening, a sign of spring. But a conversation with my elderly mother today has unsettled me.

'Things are bad,' she said over the telephone from Toronto.

I asked her what she meant.

'Oh, the world,' she said.

This time I knew what she meant without having to ask: the anger, the cruelty and violence, in the streets, on our screens. My mother is highly intuitive, overly sensitive, porous to the people and events around her, and a good barometer of others' intentions, nasty or good. She has always been a glowing, smiling presence, but recently she has seemed distant. Her short-term memory has deteriorated significantly, and I am now noticing an acceleration of the loss of things farther back. A few weeks ago, when I asked her to tell me again the story of my grandmother's rape, she didn't remember telling me about it the first time. Perhaps, now in her mid-eighties, she has suppressed the language of rape or war or racism, as she tries to remember what she's meant to do every day. Perhaps the slippery uncertainty of the here and now is more urgent than her mother running through a sugar cane field. Or perhaps my teenage imagination made more of her whispers than was real.

Still, as the stories slip from my mother's mind, they take a part of my identity with them. It feels urgent to piece them together because no single story of race has defined me.

Race *is* a story.

Throughout history, people have enslaved others using vibrant language to justify their actions. Aristotle, who lived from 384 to 322 BCE, described the Barbarians, the people enslaved by his fellow Greeks, as 'by nature incapable of reasoning … [they] live a life of pure sensation, like certain tribes on the borders of the civilised world, or like people who are diseased through the onset of illnesses like epilepsy or madness'.

In stories of war and conquest, 'savages' run riot. After centuries of conflict with the Irish, Queen Elizabeth I declared them incapable of civilisation, a convenient judgement that absolved her of the many atrocities inflicted upon the Irish by England as they annexed the island state. Ideas of 'savagery' persisted through the conquest of Ireland in the 1650s, when tens of thousands of Irish were sent as indentured servants to the English colonies in America and the 'West Indies'. Some English leaders even proposed laws that would enslave the poor in England too.

The poor, the criminal, the savage, the barbarian, the other. How does language make one person 'other' to the next? How do bodies become set apart and vilified? How did one question asked of me in a classroom in suburban Toronto engender a lifetime of possible answers?

In the seventeenth century, new narratives of difference were created in order to justify the expansion of the African slave trade into British territories in the Americas and the Caribbean. Who was born to command and who to obey? Politicians and statesmen called upon the highest principles of western classical philosophy to provide the answers. They cited Greek ideals of beauty and intelligence, and created principles of power based on them. The idea of race underpinned the trade in captured Africans to serve thriving cotton and sugar production on English plantations in the Americas. With the expansion of the slave trade and the economies that depended on it, racial difference now needed human classification. In the middle of the eighteenth century, the first published materials of 'scientific inquiry' argued that 'Negroes' were a separate species from white men and were either a product of degeneration from 'original man' or descendants from a separate creation altogether.

Influenced by a taxonomy of human beings introduced in *Systema Naturae*, first published in 1735 by Swedish botanist, zoologist and physician Carl Linnaeus, philosophers and naturalists began to make scientific distinctions among humans. Linnaeus' succinct classification of the African '*Afer* or *Africanus*' consisted of 'black, phlegmatic, relaxed. *Hair* black, frizzled. *Skin* silky. *Nose* flat. *Lips* tumid. *Women* without shame. *Mammae* lactate profusely. *Crafty,* indolent, negligent. *Anoints* himself with grease. *Governed* by caprice.'[1]

In the 1830s, anthropologists measured the crania of skeletons, collecting 'evidence' to support the superiority of Caucasian brains over Negro brains, writing the necessary new plotlines to suit their own ends. In 1854, George Gliddon, author of *Types of Mankind*, in which he argued that Negroes were closer to apes than humans, sent a copy of his book to a politician in the US South, with a note stating that he was sure the South would appreciate the book as powerful support for their 'peculiar institution' of slavery.[2]

Race is a construct, not a reality. It is an expression of power. Still, there are new stories and new acts of violence every day that reinforce the border between black and white so completely that it feels like it will never be open. I worry that this is what my mother senses, and that it is causing her to retreat, hurt by the world — taking with her the stories that have formed me.

I am a fragile map of stories told by others, told to myself, and they make up a whole person who has often been divided. Race is a construct, but the consequences of how a culture uses race are real, as is the violence committed against people for what they look like. There is violence in making a border. There is pain in being behind a wall.

A year ago, a good friend from Canada came to visit me in London. He is white and, although born in England, has lived in Canada for many decades — he has never understood my move to a place he escaped because of its deep class division and injustices. We talked about current politics and where we stood. Both deeply committed to social equality, we do not share how the world asks us to speak to those beliefs. My race and gender obviously make my experiences different, but my racial hybridity adds a further dimension that allows me to cross some borders and not others.

'You're socially white, politically black and culturally both,' he said, and I was surprised at being described so succinctly, then felt a rising distress about what he meant — that I was fragmented, unintegrated, possibly false and therefore dangerous? He thought he was affirming me, but I felt steeped in shame.

Shame splinters you. For me, it was a biting into the apple moment. In an instant I understood that I was not what I thought or wanted or projected or hoped. I was thrown out of innocence. Shame is a fall from grace.

⸻

As a child, I was quiet, cripplingly shy and often sad. I felt set apart at school and often even at home. I recall no real sense of belonging. How do we connect to a nation state, a class, a gender, a family, an occupation, an ethnicity, a religion, a football team or a club of any kind? Is belonging something given to you or something you create? While many people are turning to DNA testing to find out what they are, I expect that if I were to spit into a vial and send samples off for analysis, my DNA might cause a system outage in the lab at 23&Me. I am a kind of middle ground in the current language of belonging: mixed race, middle class, dual nationality. I embody both privilege and oppression.

My father faced early battles for our entire family, alone in Canada in the 1950s as a young mixed-race man who became a

Doctor of Veterinary Medicine. My family are 'good' immigrants, grateful for the opportunities that Canada gave us in the 1960s, welcomed into a young country that was building a labour force outside of its traditional immigration base of Europeans. My parents worked hard to be financially solvent in Toronto and as a result I had choices beyond what I might have had if we'd stayed in Guyana. I lived in Toronto, Kingston and Montreal before leaving Canada in 1999 to move to London and write my third book. I ended up staying. I am Canadian. I am also British. While there are superficial differences in the conversations about race in Britain and Canada, at the centre the issues are the same: violence, displacement, settlement, genocide, citizenship, migration, inequality and more. They are my mother's *Oh, the world*, the issues of 'us against them' that are dividing us.

The premise behind the DNA testing systems available via 23&Me or Ancestry.com is that they will reveal what you come from, and to some extent your destiny, based on your DNA. As my mother's memory fails, I wonder if this kind of revelation is more reliable than stories.

Chinese oracle bones, which date from between 1600 BC and 1050 BC, were an ancient 23&Me. Diviners used them to answer the elite's questions about health, birth and death; about crops, the weather; about the outcome of battles or simply whether a particular ancestor was causing a king's headache. The shoulder blades of ox, sheep, boars, horses and deer, or the shells of tortoises were cleaned of flesh, scraped, polished, and then diviners carved questions into them using a sharp tool. During a divination session, the bone was anointed with blood before questions were posed to ancestors. The diviner then applied such intense heat that the bone or shell cracked, and he interpreted the pattern of the fractures to answer the questions posed.

Shang Dynasty oracle bone. Source: British Library Board,
Couling-Chalfant collection, Or.7694/1595.

A bone with the power to provide answers would be useful to me now, but of course it was only storytelling. A DNA test is based on science, but its interpretations, too, are founded on stories. What does knowing give us? Surely *being* is more complicated than thinking that we know the answers. And divination and imagination often seem more powerful than science in framing how societies live. Even when people are confronted with scientific proof that race doesn't exist or that climate change is real, they believe their own stories instead.

Stories make meaning for us; they connect us or divide us.

I have been attracted to stories — around the dinner table, on the television — from as far back as I can remember, but I was not born into a family of readers. My father was interested in animals, sports and science; my mother, an accomplished pianist and an unfulfilled artist at her core, became a lover of books only after she completed a university degree in her sixties. When our family arrived in Toronto, I was three years old, my brother was one, and my sister was six. My Chinese grandmother accompanied us, and she and I shared a room in our rented house near High Park. She was the most important person in my life, essentially raising me and my siblings while my parents were at work. She was warm, loving and funny, but she rarely talked about herself; a girl who had run away from the Demerara countryside, she had not been educated beyond primary school. New to Canada, we concerned ourselves with survival and assimilation, not culture or art. After two years near High Park, we were able to afford a move to a suburban neighbourhood north of the city where mine was the only 'brown' family for miles, the closest 'others' being the Italian family a few houses down.

Hockey was central to being a Canadian and so my brother started skating at the age of five. To be part of my family meant to be dragged along to the rink at six o'clock each Saturday morning to watch him play hockey. Our job was to assimilate, and I became a keen observer in order to catch on to how Canadian life was lived. I spent my days feeling that life was elsewhere, and that if I watched astutely enough I would find it.

And then book learning arrived at our door.

I remember the day the salesman rang our bell. A man in a suit, with greasy brown hair and glasses. In my memory, he is a big man who towered over my father in our living room. My brother and I sat on the floor acting invisible, as the man discussed with my father the advantages that the twenty-four volume *Encyclopaedia Britannica* would bring to his young family and their future. Knowledge is power, he might have said as he glanced over at us on the floor. My father — a frugal man born during the Depression in British Guiana and yet a fervent believer in education as the source of all progress — signed up for a complete set. These were the only books in our house, other than those we children brought home from school, which is not an unusual story for many families. But I felt there were secrets which could be revealed through stories; there was mystery and knowledge to be had outside of my family. I made up stories I told no one, cossetting that mystery like a best friend. I had a stuffed monkey, George, to whom I spoke, telling him secrets, the way a writer tells the page.

I began to read in grade one, when I was five years old. I was behind some of the other kids — all of them white, though I had yet to identify them as such. Some of them had learned to read in kindergarten or even earlier. One day our teacher assigned us the task of presenting to the entire class a book we'd chosen from the library. After taking my book home, reading it to George after school, sharing it with no one else in my family, I arrived at school the next day ready, albeit terrified, to speak in front of the whole class. While I waited for my turn, I ran over the things in my mind that I would have to say about my book. The easy part was its title, *Island Duckling*. I knew from the book that Island must be a great place. Island, as I understood it, was where the mallard family came from. Island was easily pronounced because it was made up of two words I knew: *is* and *land*. Great, I had that nailed. The problem would be not to let my shyness get the better of me, and to speak loudly enough to tell my classmates and the teacher how the ducklings spent their day. When my turn came, my teacher introduced me and asked me to hold up my book. When she pronounced its title ('I'-land Duckling), she threw me off course so profoundly that I stuttered my way through the story and sat back down quickly, without telling them the best part, which I can't remember now, but I'm sure was about the youngest duckling's triumphs. I knew what an island was, but I had not realised that is-land and island were the same thing. I had been reading all wrong.

This early shame left its mark on my confidence. It turned out that language had tricks. I needed to find the secret. And I needed to catch up with what everyone else seemed to know already. In grade two, I did better, but I still hadn't fully grasped how language was a system with codes and rules that I needed to follow but could also break; how powerful it really was. I sensed that I needed to immerse myself in it so as not to be tricked by it, so as not to be inferior. It was finally in grade three, with the word Negro, the question from my teacher and the burrowing eyes of my classmates on me, when I knew in my body the power of language.

'What are you?'

I have been asked this repeatedly throughout my life. Not only 'Where are you really from?' and not only 'What race are your parents?' but 'What are you?'

To strangers, even friends — on some days also to myself — I am images of violence and oppression. I am the language of shame and destitution, of slavery and indenture, of rape and murder. I am images of power and privilege, of denial and shades of skin, shapes of faces. How does thinking these ways get me anywhere but grounded, ground down, belonging nowhere else but in a story?

How do I make a life from this?

Writing is a form of running.

On television shows in both North America and Europe, people ask each other and themselves *Who Do You Think You Are?* and other variants of this question. In some of these shows, celebrities go on a journey through genetic testing and archival records to find their roots. In recent versions, members of the audience undergo genetic testing and are given the surprise results that are supposed to somehow temper preconceived notions about ethnicity and racial background.

Finding Your Roots, the celebrity genealogy show on PBS, features Harvard professor Henry Louis Gates, Jr. guiding his guests back in time towards their ancestors. In 2015, the show followed Ben Affleck and his quest to find the roots of his family's interest in social justice. The episode aired without including the information that Affleck's ancestors owned slaves, which sparked a controversy about whether Gates had suppressed information due to pressure from Affleck. A leaked email from Gates to the show's executive showed that he had sought advice about how to handle Affleck's objection to airing the slavery segment. These emails were part of the infamously hacked Sony files that were exposed by Wikileaks. An investigation at PBS ensued, and the network eventually published its findings, which confirmed that there was evidence of 'improper influence in the editorial process'. Gates and Affleck both apologised, but the irony of a rich, white movie star pressuring an influential black academic to suppress the star's slave-owning ancestry is glaring.

I feel we are now at a crossroad: a new moment of reckoning in which the economy, the environment, technology and our social lives are colliding — an urgent moment of many walls and few bridges, of history repeating and identities galvanising. I feel uneasy, and I know my colleagues, friends and family do too. What is real? What is true? I want to excavate the stories my mother once told me: to investigate why some things are suppressed and not others. I want to throw myself into the gaps, the subtext and the lost characters of my own history.

Public documents only go so far in helping me unearth the missing links in the McWatt and Eyre lineage. I want to resist reducing my search to biology, but the technology is enticing. I have ordered two DNA kits, one from 23&Me and the other from Ancestry.com. In the meantime, I hold on to my mother's days along with her, trying to understand why we are all so on edge. Known for my peaceful disposition, recently I have found myself irritable and angry at what is taking place around race. I want to dismantle the stories related to my body to understand why we still speak of and see race: to uncover how I have benefitted from some stories and not others, and to trace the suffering that comes when language is used against us.

I write now to examine what I am physically — eyes, nose, blood, hair — in relation to what I am as a person, to place myself under the microscope, to experiment, to untangle myth from skin and bone. When people ask me what race I am, I say 'writer'. Black, white, brown, yellow, red: these words I also place under scrutiny. Black is related to a body, but blackness seems something else entirely. White is related to skin colour, but whiteness is a state of mind. Shame is a way of talking about them both in the same breath. The colours themselves are meaningless to define a person. I use them here with invisible scare quotes, always aware that language is glassy and deep like a frozen lake. Language is trickery. Language is insufficient and yet ample. Language is powerful and painful.

What am I?

What are you?

ANALYSIS

1

Nose

It came upon me slowly, like that strange
disease that affects those black men whom
you see turning slowly from black to albino,
their pigment disappearing as under the
radiation of some cruel, invisible ray.

Lamb curry stewing in a pot in my mother's kitchen. Spring earth
as it emerges from beneath melting snow. My lover's breath beneath
the sheet. Frangipani in southern air; wisteria in northern air. Garlic.

These things come to us through our nose, the gateway to the
olfactory bulb at the front of the brain. Without a nose we would
still smell, but the air we inhale would not be warmed and moist-
ened, and particles in it would have a better chance of invading our
lungs. The nose is useful. Always there in the middle of our faces.
Often beautiful. But it also gets blocked, it bleeds and is a channel
for streaming mucous. It is connected to our tears.

In literature, noses often denote character, a feature on a face to
mock, to pity, to scorn, like Pinocchio's, Cyrano's, Tristam Shandy's,

Shylock's. The poor nose has been used as a sign of weakness, a stand-in for the penis; the poor nose has been racialised and ridiculed.

Many cultures at different moments in history have searched the face for clues to explain character and personality. There are physiognomies from ancient Greece, Chinese astrology and nineteenth-century Italy that all claim to 'reveal' the character or spirit of a person, based on features, colour, size. In ancient Greece, a physiognomist claimed that Socrates was sensuous and hot-headed. In Chinese face-reading, the nose is related to wealth — it is considered difficult for a person with an upturned nose to make a fortune, while a garlic bulb nose is a positive sign of wealth. And in the nineteenth century, Italian criminologist and scientist Cesare Lombroso analysed living bodies, cadavers, skulls, tattoos, height, weight, strength and the shapes of noses, ears, foreheads, even the way someone spoke, for evidence of the 'criminal type'. He claimed that criminals were born, not made.

Meanwhile, in nineteenth-century Britain, physiognomy and phrenology were both popular ways of looking at human action, interaction and difference. From the 1820s to 1840s, many employers would demand that their potential employees obtain a character reference from a local phrenologist in order to prove their honesty and ability to work hard. The influence of those pseudo-sciences waned after Darwin published *On the Origin of Species*, which demonstrated that evolution, and not God, was the source of human diversity.

In his *Notes on Noses*, published in 1852, George Jabet argued for a classification of noses that opposed the phrenologist's view that the body affects the mind. Jabet believed that the 'Mind forms the Nose' and not the other way around. He classified noses based on cognitive abilities, and also included interpretations of ethnicity. The 'superior' mind of the classical ideal was expressed by the Roman and Greek, aquiline and straight noses. He believed that a person could develop a 'cogitative' nose (a classical nose but with wider nostrils) by rigorous training of the mind. He described the 'Jewish' hook nose (shrewdness with money), the snub nose (natural weakness; mean, disagreeable, disposition; with petty insolence), the feminine nose ('The Cogitative Nose does not so frequently appear among women as among men. Women rather feel than think. Their perceptions are instinctive, intuitive; men's cogitative') and a host of 'national' noses, all conforming to the stereotypes of the day, in relation to the English ideal. Always there, in the middle of our faces.

In my family when I was a child, noses — their size, whose they resemble, what line of the family they come from and how they suit the rest of our faces — were regular topics of conversation. Not in any scientific sense, but because of the complexity of our genetic history, they became story points.

My London cousin has sent me photos.

In my search for something concrete to substantiate my mother's stories, I have been in touch with him about our family tree. Among the photos is one of my paternal great-grandfather at what appears to be a Sunday family gathering in British Guiana. It's a faded, torn black-and-white, dating from — going by the hairstyles — the late 1930s, when my great-grandfather, born in 1860, would have been nearly eighty. His hair is white, his face obscured by the faded grain of the photograph, but I scrutinise it for a resemblance to my dad or anyone else in our family. I can't get a clear enough view, but this man with a Scottish surname is black with a wide nose, prominent cheek bones and a long face.

My great-grandfather, Richard Hendricks McWatt, and family.
Source: Family photo.

In another, yellowed photo, his son, my grandfather, who worked as a bookkeeper at the West India Oil Company, is seated inside a Morris Saloon from the early 1930s. Six of his seven children, including my father, are perched on the running board of the car, with my grandmother standing beside them. These faces are lighter shades than those in the first photo. My grandmother's family was French Creole with, according to my mother, a rumour of Jewish blood. My dad, his brothers and sister are brown, one brother with fair hair, and another who looks distinctly Indian.

My grandfather, Richard Alexander McWatt, and my grandmother, Henrietta (Hetta) Wilhelmina Cendrecourt, and six of their seven children. My father is fourth from the left. Source: Family photo.

I sift through more photos and find one of my grand-aunt, one of my mother's English 'mulatto' and 'buck' father — the Eyre whom I had once imagined to be a relative of Jane's — and one of my uncle's wife standing with my Chinese grandmother. Another is of my older cousins as toddlers, before I was born: brown faces, brown eyes, unchiselled features, uncategorisable. I find fragments of myself in them. I notice that included in the shot is my brother, the first born, looking off into the distance while his cousin tries to turn his face towards the camera.

Above, left: My grand-aunt, Josephine Cendrecourt. Source: Family photo.

Right: My grandfather, Donald Oscar Patrick Eyre. Source: Family photo.

Mr. D. O. P. Eyre
Director, G. R.
Hutchison, Ltd.

Above, left: My aunt,
Dorothy Margaret
Sharples, and my
grandmother, Anna
Beatrice Eyre (née
"Lenchay" Lena Yuk
Layne). Source: Family
photo.

Right: My brother,
Charles, at the wheel,
and some of my cousins.
Source: Family photo.

The photos fill me with longing — for my grandmother, whom even my mother will admit did all the mothering of me — and they bring back a familiar sadness that lies deep in the bosom of our family.

In the British Guiana that they left behind, my mother and father, his five brothers and one sister and their families lived close to one another on a compound in Kitty, a neighbourhood in Georgetown. My cousins have regaled me with light-hearted stories of their childhood shenanigans, the tricks they played on adults and each other. One recounted being dragged to Temperance League meetings at the YMCA by our paternal grandmother and made to sing, 'Alcohol is like a burglar, never let him in'. These cousins, aunts, uncles, in-laws and grandparents shared daily woes or triumphs, looked after the children together, celebrated holidays, births and marriages, and supported one another through losses.

My parents' first child, the boy in the photo looking off into the distance, died after a short illness when he was three years old, not too long after this photo was taken. My sister had already been born, and the three of them, along with this extended family, grieved deeply for the loss of this bright light. My mother, I was told, sat over his grave and would not leave as the rain started to fall, wanting to protect him from it, declaring through tears that she could not let him get wet. Eventually, my father pulled her up and away from the graveside.

My father grieved more silently, but my mother's grief is still palpable. Along with the loss of her son, my mother also had to cope with her own father's nervous breakdown. As the country became embroiled in racial tensions during the early 1960s, he was hospitalised in a mental asylum in Berbice — The Berbice Mad House, as it was and is still known.

In the 1950s and 60s in many countries, depression and mental illness were matters for the asylum, were treated by electroconvulsive therapy (ECT) and straitjackets; people who fell ill were isolated and stigmatised. My mother described her attempt to visit her father in the asylum, how she arrived at the gate and heard screams from behind the walls that stopped her short. She struggled with the heartache of bringing my grandmother with us to Toronto and leaving him behind.

My mother covers her anxiety with smiles, but she hates hospitals and will not go to funerals. I imagine that the image of her three-year-old son dying in a hospital cot causes her to worry about illness for all of us, her grown children, even to this day. Throughout my childhood, every Christmas Eve, I stood silently at the door to our living room, not wanting to disturb her, as she lay on the floor next to the Christmas tree, crying.

I was the only planned child in the family, the conscious replacement for the lost child. Yet my parents' grief didn't have space for me, and my grandmother took over my care. My infant self must have interpreted my parents' grief as my fault. I was a good child, an obedient and responsive little girl who did everything she was told, who loved extra hard when others were neglectful or nasty, who made special Christmas cards and decorations, who heard and appreciated both sides of an argument, who strove to alleviate pain. But my inability to console my mother, and her inability to trust that she could nurture a child who wouldn't be taken from her, became for me a colossal failure.

British Guiana in the early 1960s was a volatile, violent place, riven by racial tension between those of Indian and African heritage, who were represented by rival political parties. Middle-class, mixed race people, like my family, were targeted — their houses burned down — and many began to leave the country. Ethnic riots broke out in February 1962, forcing the Prime Minister to declare a state of emergency, and two thousand British troops were deployed to suppress the riots. In one violent street demonstration, my five-year-old sister's face was cut by a straw broom waved by a supporter of the party whose motto it was to 'sweep out' the decadence of the legacy of the white planter class. The cut on my sister's face was the last straw for my father, and he decided that we had to leave. As much as he loved his country of birth, his career, his extended family and friends, he felt forced to find a life elsewhere.

The asylum, the ECT, the screams, the fire, the straw broom, the bloody cheek: these images are fixed in my imagination.

There was madness in the street, yes, but there was also madness deep inside Britain's colonial subjects. The Guyanese version of colonialism consisted of a tiny, European planter class that dominated not only the indigenous people who had survived slaughter by earlier conquerors, but also the enslaved Africans and the Indian and Chinese indentured labourers who arrived over decades to work on their plantations. There was madness in a system that transported people from four continents, forced them into intimacy around a single crop that would be sold to the world, and yet omitted them from the success story of Demerara sugar.

In the 1950s, as post-war independence movements took hold, the country suffered an identity crisis and there was nowhere for my grandfather to belong. He broke down. When he was released from hospital, he moved to Toronto to live with us, but he and my grandmother were never a couple again. In the small house where I shared a room with his wife, a room he never entered, my grandfather seemed embattled. He relegated himself in the evenings to the room my father built for him in the basement. I used to sneak past him as he sat on the couch in our living room, staring down into his lap or at his feet. I wondered what it was that he did with his day, what he thought about, who he really was. I knew he had been in a mental asylum and that frightened me. Later, when I had the right words, I began to think of him as the quintessential colonial subject, his white and black and indigenous body silenced by the madness of colonialism.

The madness of sugar.

When we moved to Canada, my father left the house at five o'clock every morning to drive downtown to the meat processing plant where he was the veterinarian in charge of meat inspection, a job that disappointed him after his work as district veterinarian in British Guiana. When I was older, I understood that he had been regularly subjected to veiled racist jibes and overlooked for promotion by the plant's owners. My mother worked as a secretary to supplement my father's income, as they were not only supporting our family but also her parents. And at home I was entranced by my caring grandmother, who sang over the sound of running water at the sink while she did the dishes and looked out of the window in front of her. She gave me melodies that were the soundtrack of menial tasks: 'When you walk through a storm,' she sang, her voice steady and lonely in the small kitchen. She spoke only rarely to my grandfather, usually to call him for dinner or to say goodnight as she retreated to the room she shared with me. The storm she was walking through was more complicated than I could understand.

My grandfather and I never conversed much, but I remember him reading the *Encyclopaedia Britannica*, volume after volume, over many years. From him I learned a habit of concentration and focus that became a source of solace.

As a teenager — still not knowing the answer to 'What are you?' — I began to devour books: in particular, those with characters who questioned what it was to be alive, books in which protagonists sought to be free by any means necessary. Suddenly I was an existentialist. At sixteen, I read Camus' *The Stranger* and Dostoyevsky's *Notes from Underground* and didn't find them bleak. With their blunt, honest depictions of how a false life in false systems prevents true human freedom and creativity, these novels propelled me towards my essential self, which was inherently free if only I could escape the perception of others. Society was full of falsities; those who saw themselves as outsiders could be united in their disdain for the mainstream, and I was one of them. I also became obsessed with the work of Herman Hesse, finding spiritual solace in the tenets of Buddhism. I saw no contradiction between the stark realities of existentialism and the history, philosophy and practice of Buddhism. What I shared with these foreign white male writers was a belonging that was beyond the physical realities of a body.

I did not know then that only white males are allowed to exist outside of their bodies.

I had leapt, without understanding what I was doing, beyond race. While my parents worked hard to give us a better life, my siblings and I strove to become successful, unconsciously absorbing our father's unhappiness in his job, and aware of the sacrifices they were making for us. My true aspiration, though, became to leave behind the questions of what my body represented to others.

Our high school had a majority of Jewish students. Everyone in the school had holidays at Rosh Hashanah and Yom Kippur. I didn't fully understand the importance of the holidays, but of course was happy for the days off, on which I felt I was participating in something significant, as well as mysterious and 'other', in a way that my elementary school experience had failed to provide. The lessons from history class I remember the clearest were those about the Second World War. I was most moved by the painful horror of stories around the Holocaust; I read *The Diary of Anne Frank*, and felt connected to my schoolmates in a way that I never articulated or even analysed for myself. We didn't study British colonialism so much as Canada's British heritage, the struggles with 'French Canada' and the growth of the dominion. We learned about various indigenous peoples who were on the land during the fur trade and the shaping of Upper and Lower Canada, but the genocide of First Nations people was mostly a footnote.

My closest friends and I called ourselves the United Nations. We were Hungarian, Latvian, Jewish, Japanese and Caribbean. We were the in-betweeners of our time, revelling in the post-hippie vibe of the 1970s and feeling part of a trajectory that would see us all become 'one'. This oneness was symbolised in the crudest way in the growing consumerism of the time. We drank Coca Cola, but we did so in the spirit of the 'I'd Like to Teach the World to Sing' ad that showed people united on a grassy knoll, singing, one at a time towards a chorus of unity. I felt ahead of this game, given that mine was a bloodline that spelled the future: like my family, the world would become blended.

The school had a strong reputation for sports, particularly track and field, and during my time several young men from Caribbean backgrounds would go on to become part of Canada's Olympic team. The affinity I felt to them was not in skin colour but in speed. I was on the relay team and did well in the 100 metres. I also excelled at the high jump, earning a record in my age group for the district that lasted long after I finished high school. I spent May and June afternoons on the track, and after practice lounging in the high-jump pit with the boys. My coach and others on the team encouraged a relationship between me and one of the fastest runners, primarily, I see now, because they thought we looked good together. While I enjoyed hanging out in the pit because I felt like one of the boys, athletic and happy using my body, I wasn't seeking a relationship. I loved the long June days when the grass sang with insects in the perfect heat.

Still, the fast runner and I felt pressured into dating. He was beautiful, kind, from a Barbadian background. He took me to dinner, and we established a weekly outing with others to local clubs, faking our way into bars with our teammates, doing the hustle like the dancers on *Soul Train*.

By now, my grandmother had moved to a senior's apartment on her own, and when I visited her after school every day, I told her things about my life — not about the underage drinking and dancing, but about my new boyfriend. In Canada, Caribbean people from different nations liked to huddle together in solidarity against the cold, so I proudly told her his parents were born in Barbados. She looked into my face for a few brief seconds and nodded, then she asked me if they were black. Yes, I said, and went on to describe what a good runner he was and how his friend on the team had been scouted for the Olympics. But she changed the subject, which was unusual between us.

I thought she'd forgotten about him, when a few days later she put some chow mein on the kitchen table in front of me and sat down opposite.

'You mustn't marry a black man,' she said.

I stopped my dive into the dish and looked up. Is that what I was doing? In that moment it wasn't so much her racism that horrified me, but that having a boyfriend would somehow result in marriage.

'It would be going backwards,' she said, and stood up again, humming the tune she hummed while doing the dishes: 'Hold your head up high, and don't be afraid of the dark. At the end of the storm ...'

I felt my cheeks burn. I pushed the noodles around on the plate, picking out small pieces of chicken and placing them to the side as though stockpiling them for later.

My grandmother's reaction to my boyfriend's race was colonial, and backward, but we have not come very far. We assign values to some people's lives over others; we believe in narratives of progress that leave many behind. Rich, powerful countries declare they are full;

migrants drown in the sea. Political leaders tweet and give speeches about putting 'us' first. Black men the same age as the fast runner I dated are shot or tasered or arrested in the street.

Bodies running.

The runner and I broke up after a month, not because of what my grandmother said, but because we discovered that we had little in common. I was more in love with the minds of the writers I was reading. I was also in love with James Taylor, Carole King, and the roaming, earthy ballads of folk music. Joni Mitchell was the heroine of women like me, who wanted to be free, wanted to hitchhike to the coast to stand on a rock with the lick of salt air from the Pacific Ocean on our cheeks. Women who questioned the desire to commit to any one man. I had yet to understand just who was allowed this kind of freedom.

In this quest for understanding — a quest for my own freedom — I already knew that the contradictions of colour, the lack of belonging, could be made intelligible by words. The process of writing, the escape into my imagination, allowed me to disappear, like I had into my arms on the desk as an eight-year-old.

My mother hates England. I've lived here for over two decades, and she has persistently refused my invitations to visit. On her only trip to Europe — in 1956, pregnant with my sister, vomiting in her cabin on the RMS *Queen Elizabeth*, vomiting in the car with my father and their travelling companions on the journey from Southampton — she arrived at boarding houses where they had a booking, only to be turned away when the proprietors saw the clearly not-Scottish McWatts on their doorstep. She describes nights when she had to sleep on my father's coat laid on top of straw in a barn in France, again having been turned away from *pensions* and small hotels. At a restaurant in Paris they sat for over an hour while bored waiters passed by, even stood next to them, and never took their order.

She tells these stories with irony and humour, but there is a wound at the core of them. In one, she and my father are strolling through Hyde Park. They walk towards Speakers' Corner, at the northeast edge of the park, near what was once the site of public hangings at Tyburn Gallows where the condemned were given their chance to make a final speech. After the gallows were dismantled, and demonstrators in the 1870s demanded free use of the park, the corner became a regular spot for public rallies and political speeches. Decades later it became famous as a spot for individuals — including civil rights leader Marcus Garvey and the Trinidadian social theorist C. L. R. James — to speak out about any and everything.

As my parents reach the small crowd at the corner, they tune in to the loud, Jamaican accent of a black man who is waving his hands about as he proclaims his truths. He speaks about his homeland — sunshine and good food, he emphasises — as the crowd begins to grow. He describes what it is like for him, a man from the tropics, to have arrived in this cold country. Change is coming, he insists. The world cannot stay the same.

He gestures to the crowd of mostly white people, their faces amused and full of disdain. 'Ysee all ya? All ya people here?' The man sweeps his hand around in a semi-circle in front of him, across the throng of faces. 'See y'all white people? We gwon brown y'all up!'

My mother laughs when she tells this story. When I first heard it, I could not hear the undertone of rage in the man's words. Her laugh obscured the threat the rest of the crowd likely carried home with them; as a child I took the man's words to mean that we would soon all live in harmony.

My brother and sister experienced our 1970s suburban upbringing differently than I did. Though we resemble one another, we are the various components of our ancestors in different proportions. My sister, in racialised terms, is the most 'fair', and she was the tallest among the girls and most of the boys in school. She was beautiful and not shy like me. When she was in grade five a boy named Stephen who had a crush on her (as she did on him) kicked her in the leg, pushed her down in the snow and called her 'nigger' in front of his friends. She recalls this as the moment in which she became resolved to let nothing stand in her way.

My brother, who looked more like me than my sister did, experienced more brutal racism. As a hockey player he was often cornered, battered, called 'nigger' as he was jabbed with a stick while he played his heart out to become a good Canadian. The physical violence was in the name of sport, but he knew the jabs and the spit that flew through mouth guards to hit his face were not about the game. The hockey players he faced had no desire to 'teach the world to sing'. That dream was still only in a bottle of Coca Cola, that song of sugar whose mass consumption was only ever possible thanks to slavery.

Sugar makes us happy, giddy, fat. It is the central ingredient in cheap, processed food, contributing to obesity, diabetes and other health problems. Introduced into the daily diet of Britons as a result of high yields on British sugar plantations in the 'West Indies', sugar's proliferation during the slave trade, and the reliance on cheap labour to produce it, are symbolic of current inequalities. The plantation was a model for a modern factory: a workplace of unequals, a site upon which near magical technology would turn cane to crystals, in an export enterprise that would yield its owners millions of pounds or francs or guilders. The plantation's wealth relied on its structure being *by necessity* racist. Like a predator and its victim, richness and poverty remain in a state of perpetual chase. While slavery was abolished, the structure that produced it still flourishes.

I imagine a sugar plantation in British Guiana in the 1850s, twenty years after the abolition of slavery. Order has collapsed; productivity suffers. Freed Africans choose not to continue the backbreaking work they had endured while enslaved. With Demerara now firmly in the hands of the British, after successive European wars over the colonies, British planters in the region urgently need workers.

New ships, with different cargo, arrive: a succession of labourers to fill the quota on this plantation. They are poor people working to pay off debt, or those who have no other options, who sign contracts of indenture to work for a fixed period. Some have been promised land in the new colony at the end of their contracts.

Portuguese people from Madeira, struck by famine, are the first to be offered such contracts: 17,098 men and women go to British Guiana between 1835 and 1850. The colonial government's theory is that white labourers will help to create a little bit of Europe in the country. But the Portuguese die in unprecedented numbers doing work they have no experience in, under difficult conditions.

Indians are recruited next, people more used to the climate, drawn from both Madras and Calcutta, though soon the labourers from Madras get a reputation for falling sick and deserting, and for being more difficult to manage. It is almost impossible to recruit single women, and so the authorities attempt to entice whole families. Sickness *en route* and upon arrival prevails. The mortality rate during the wet season is high. Malaria is rampant. But the extreme poverty in India, where wages are 8–10 cents a day, and the relative prosperity in British Guiana, where an able bodied and energetic immigrant earns never less than 30 cents a day, ensures a steady flow of workers — in total 238,909 during the period of indenture between 1844 and 1916.

The contract obliges a person to work nine hours a day for up to six days a week and to live on the estate. If they are found more than two miles from their plantation on weekdays without a pass, they are likely to be arrested, fined and possibly imprisoned. Many of these 'coolies' die in their first year due to the harsh conditions. The 'coolie bounty' — their advance payment upon signing a contract — is difficult to pay off. If they do survive their legal length of service of five years, they are often forced to work another three years before they can afford to buy their freedom.

Sugar production flourishes, and Demerara sugar is exported around the world. But contracts run out, desertion and illness are still rampant, and workers from India are much more expensive than enslaved Africans. In 1853, colonial authorities target cheaper

Chinese immigrants, who wish to escape war and rebellion in that country's southern provinces. Out of the 13,541 who arrive between 1853 and 1879 on the ship *Whirlwind*, only 2,975 are women. Again, many fall ill and die in the early stages of their contract, but those who survive are efficient workers.

Researchers come from Britain, from India, from America to document the magic of the plantation and the sugar it produces, to marvel at the technology, the plant biology, the machinery of sugar. In detailed drawings of the plantation works, illustrators pay intricate, intimate attention to the ingenio that 'grinds or squeezes' the sugar, perfectly depicting the cogs. The text accompanying the drawings describes how the 'juice of the Cane' is conveyed by pipes to the boiling house where it is made to simmer with a 'judicious application' of heat. But the illustrators do not convey anywhere near such excitement when they draw the people involved. An overseer holds a whip. A man carries a load. Other brown bodies are at work among the cogs. Nothing to see here. Just a factory.

I came across a book-length poem called *The Sugar Cane*, by James Grainger, published in 1764, which is a detailed, extensive poetic treatment of the sugar crop — the soil, the conditions needed for planting and cultivating, the threats to growth, the harvesting and boiling processes — yet has little to say about who is responsible for the work. While in a neutral voice Grainger mentions 'Afric's sable progeny', he extolls the planter's profits with exuberance: 'Thrice happy he, to whom such fields are given! / For him the Cane with little labour grows.' He does not describe field workers bent over the soil, planting at daybreak, pulling weeds, their battered hands weak from wielding cutlasses, their backs weighed down by the loads of cane they carry to the ingenio under the hot sun.

Demerara sugar is famous. The 'cargo' transported from many corners of the world to harvest and process it is erased.

Slave labour on a sugar plantation in the West Indies. From P. Pomet, 'A Compleat History of Drugs', 1725. Source: World History Archive / Alamy Stock Photo.

In British Guiana, there is a pyramid of colour that represents status, with white at the top, other Europeans and fair-skinned mulattos next, then Chinese, then Indian, then African at the bottom. Those remaining indigenous people whose ancestors survived the systematic slaughter during earlier colonial 'conquests' are so disregarded as to not have a place in the pyramid at all.

I can't leave out the planter. The master. Perhaps I am not related to him personally. The evidence in my family's search for

Scottish origins suggests that my great-great grandfather McWatt was related to overseers rather than owners. But the hierarchy is self-evident, and it would have allowed the overseer, as the planter's representative, easy access to the mechanisms of power: to whips, knives, chains, fire.

And sex.

The McWatt database, on Ancestry.com, put together by willing researchers around the world, is a family tree with many branches and many offspring, with some branches traced back to ancestors in East Lothian in Scotland, who left to work on plantations in Berbice and Demerara. But there is no mention on the database of the black woman with whom my white great-great grandfather had a child who took his name. No birth, no death, no marriage recorded. With more sleuthing I might be able to trace her, but it is the fact that the tree goes from white to black without explanation that interests me most. It is the gap, the invisibility that I sank into that day in grade three when I did not know the answer to 'What are you?'

'You go along for years knowing something is wrong, then suddenly you discover that you're as transparent as air. At first you tell yourself that it's all a dirty joke, or that it's due to the "political situation",' says Ralph Ellison's protagonist in *Invisible Man*. The 'Man' was one of the first black characters in literature that I identified with. Ellison too was influenced by the existentialists; his narrator searches for an authentic self, which he can't find in a society structured on race, and so he retreats underground. At the opening of the novel, he is living in a hole beneath the city, stealing electricity from the power company and waiting for his moment to resurface into a world that has betrayed him. His invisibility, he says, comes from a way of seeing and yet not seeing. It comes from assumptions about him, and about what humans are. In his life before the hole, he takes part in one of the most devastating encounters I have ever read.

As a star pupil at a school for black children, he makes a graduation speech in which he asserts that humility is the secret, the very essence of progress. He is then invited to give this speech at a gathering of the town's leading white citizens. Before delivering the speech, however, he is forced to participate in a boxing match with other young black boys. They are blindfolded, set against one another and humiliated by the white spectators who goad them to obliterate their opponents in the ring. The spectators bet on the outcomes, choose favourites, push one towards the other, since the boys can't see who they are fighting. Throughout the ordeal our narrator thinks of the speech he must deliver after the battle and tries to hold it in his memory. He is hurt and hurts others too. Finally, when the bell rings and the fight is over, the spectators throw money onto an electrified carpet and make the boys, still blindfolded, scramble on hands and knees for it. Our narrator's face is bruised and swollen, his mouth bleeding, and as he delivers his speech he has to pause to swallow blood. At one point he is interrupted and ridiculed for his use of the words 'social responsibility'. When asked to repeat himself he accidently says 'equality' instead of responsibility, enraging the crowd, who force him to apologise.

The Man is expelled from the school. He goes to New York, is betrayed and challenged there too, and yet finds his place among people who put his exceptional oratorical powers to use. In Harlem he strives to alleviate social strife, and along the way learns lessons of loyalty, justice, and the true role of race in a power structure. But in the end, broken by the sight of a black comrade selling 'Sambo' dolls, and betrayed by the self-serving racism of the communist Brotherhood, he retreats underground. In the epilogue, we return to his light-filled hole beneath the city:

> But deep down you come to suspect that you're
> yourself to blame, and you stand naked and shivering
> before the millions of eyes who look through you
> unseeingly. *That* is the real soul-sickness ...

In my twenties, this novel, along with Frantz Fanon's *Black Skin, White Masks* appealed to me because they spoke of the power dynamics that create race as a psychological undertaking that I too was embroiled in. Fanon was a psychiatrist, and his analysis of anti-black racism mirrored what I saw as the madness of colonialism, the same 'sugar madness' my grandfather suffered. Fanon traces the consequences of colonialism on the colonised and the coloniser. He analyses whiteness and blackness, skin and masks, and forces us to look at what lies beneath them. He comes to the conclusion that he has only one duty:

> That of demanding human behavior from the other.
> One duty alone: That of not renouncing my freedom

through my choices ... There is no white world,
there is no white ethic, any more than there is a white
intelligence. There are in every part of the world men
who search.

But history interrupted Ellison's and Fanon's individual, exis-
tential freedom. *Invisible Man* and *Black Skin, White Masks* (both
published in 1952) were written during the intellectual bourgeoning
that led to civil rights activism in the United States. Black essential-
ism and the négritude movement around the world — a primarily
literary movement founded by black intellectuals, particularly Aimé
Césaire, in Paris during the 1920s and 30s — were grounded in a
rejection of colonialism, an affirmation to 'decolonise the mind' of
the black writer and to embrace blackness as powerful. The black
radicalism of the 1950s that promised to free these writers and artists
through collective radical action was supplanted in the US by the
civil rights movement that strove for integration — an integration
that has never truly arrived and has never dismantled the structural
inequality of the plantation.

In my reveries of harmony as a teenager, I genuinely believed
I was part of something new. *Fool me once, shame on you.* I was
focussed on authenticity, but did not take into account my invisible
African ancestor. I did not directly associate myself with the négritude movement, because I assumed that the so-called Radical Sixties
had broken down the barriers, had integrated us, and made us all
free. I focussed on what Fanon says about the individual. It was my
responsibility to become my own future:

The disaster of the man of color lies in the fact that he was enslaved. The disaster and the inhumanity of the white man lie in the fact that somewhere he has killed man …

I, the man of color, want only this:

That the tool never possess the man. That the enslavement of man by man cease forever. That is, of one by another. That it be possible for me to discover and to love man, wherever he may be.

The Negro is not. Any more than the white man …

My final prayer: O my body, make of me always a man who questions!

In the life our family was aspiring to lead in our suburb in Toronto I lobbied keenly for the things that would help me to belong: the clothes, the bicycle, swimming goggles. And pets. Although my father was a veterinarian, he was a specialist in horses and other live-stock, not small animals. He didn't particularly like cats, and believed that dogs were meant to live outside. I wanted a toy-poodle puppy just like the one my friends down the road were given for Christmas. After much badgering from us, my parents gave in to the idea of a dog, but when my dad showed up with it, I was never more disap-pointed in my life. He brought a stray mutt, a miniature Chihuahua and Manchester Terrier crossbreed to join our mutt family.

I wanted better clothes than the ones we were dressed in, which were a mishmash from Honest Ed's bargain store and the local plaza shops. While we were relatively privileged, I wanted more privilege. I didn't understand then that I was learning to simply want more, whatever it was.

It's past midnight on an August night the year I am ten. My brother, sister and I stand in front of the mirror in the bathroom of our house in Willowdale. We are too excited to sleep, because in the morning we are going for the first time on an airplane, on holiday to Barbados. We giggle in front of the mirror, pulling faces, and one of us — I can't remember who — decides we should measure our noses to see who has the biggest one. We laugh through the whole exercise of measuring, which we perform with a comb, counting the number of teeth needed to span each nose. When we laugh, our noses spread, making them appear bigger, so we have to keep a straight face in order to win, which each of us is determined to do. Though my sister is obviously the one with the smallest, most 'Caucasian' nose, we play the game nevertheless, my brother and I battling it out for second place. The results are inconclusive due to the laughing, but we're both adamant that our nose is the smaller of the two.

In the hierarchy of status and privilege on the plantation, a small nose would have marked our proximity to whiteness, and would have been advantageous.

Our unspoken family project as immigrants in Toronto was to become Canadian, which at the time was defined by a hierarchy that prized the same classical ideals in noses as nineteenth century physiognomists. Since our survival depended on belonging, having less of a nose meant having more access to success; and success was a way to be loved.

In today's racism, bodies are still interpreted for their worth. Boats have new cargo. The migrant and refugee crisis have 'race' and otherness at their core. Borders have closed. Bodies are still at risk just for being what they are.

The multicultural image of people standing on a grassy knoll singing in unison has been refurbished in advertisements over the years from Benetton, Nike and Pepsi. A few years ago, a Pepsi advertisement created controversy by mimicking a Black Lives Matter moment in which a crowd of young people of colour are in a standoff with police. A young woman — Kendall Jenner, a high-profile model — joins the crowd and heads to the front of the line to hand an enraged policeman a can of Pepsi. The crowd cheer, the policeman takes a sip and smiles. Unity, peace and understanding.

My stomach churned when I first saw this, not only because I was ashamed at having once been fooled. But also because Jenner and her social media star family, the Kardashians, are renowned for their use of cosmetics and surgery to 'black-face' their way into a kind of 'desirable blackness' that suits the Instagram era. Pepsi chose to use a non-black woman for their advertisement mimicking the Black Lives Matter movement. Resistance to this ad forced Pepsi to pull it, but, still, it demonstrated just how the language of resistance has been and can be appropriated. It left us with only a false image, not the reality. With race at the centre of commodification. Plain as the nose on your face.

Illustrations of the Caucasian race. Source: Wellcome Collection CC BY.

2

Lips

**For I know that house where I will be
cold and not belonging ... In that bed
I will dream the end of my dream.**

By way of my lips I taste food, water, and you in a kiss. Lips bring us
to one another, through smiles, through touch, but also through the
language they construct with sound. Lips are our keys to intimacy.
They are also emblems of beauty, desire and power.

The Mursi and Surma women of Ethiopia are known for the
clay or wood discs they insert into their lower lips. The Sara and
Lobi women of Chad and the Makonde of Tanzania and Mozambique
wear upper-lip plates for a variety of economic and social-status
reasons. These lip plates are symbols of achievement, are markers of
rites of passage, are both aesthetic expression and a show of strength.

Here, in South America, where I have come to spend Easter
with my cousins in Guyana, lip plates are associated with marriage
among indigenous people in the Amazon basin. Among the senior
men of the Kayapo in Brazil, the saucer-sized disc — six centimetres

across — that they wear in the lower lip represents social maturity, but also oratory prowess.

Lips are resilient.

A bird comes to the window of my cousin's house in Georgetown and perches on the edge of the Demerara shutter. It has brown wing feathers, a yellow breast and a white band above its eyes that makes it look like a bandit. It is a common bird in South America, known for its onomatopoeic call. *Kiss, kiss, kiss ka dee* it sings on the wooden shutter, unafraid of me as I hold my breath, hoping it will stay.

My mother has talked about this bird throughout my life. 'Kiss ka dee, kiss ka dee,' she will sing, becoming a girl again. She will whistle other songs, but my mother is a terrible whistler. As a child I must have been more attuned to her grief than her laughter, because I thought she didn't know how to whistle. Despite her grief, I now know she is a woman who cannot keep a straight face; her full-bow lips always part in a smile that is fixed deep in her heart. It's why *kiss ka dee* works for her; it's a song that requires a smile.

Today's bird is anxious, as though warning me not to get swept up in the sweaty bustle that is Georgetown, to stay in and gather my thoughts about the trip we have just returned from, which took us in a twelve-seater Cessna airplane over the rainforest and the brown rivers of north-western Guyana, to the settlement of Mabaruma, near the border with Venezuela.

I have come to Guyana for a holiday and also to research the 'what' of my inheritance. It will be two years this coming summer since my father died, and I never thought I'd have reason to visit our

birth country again after I came here with him twenty-five years ago.
I had been in Georgetown only that once since leaving at the age
of three, but this trip feels urgent. When I called my mother to tell
her about the trip, which I'd planned to coincide with my London
cousin's so that he could fill in some gaps about our family, she'd been
confused, sure that I was going to be in Toronto with her for Easter.
I reminded her that I had always planned to visit her in summer, not
Easter. I could hear the intake of breath as she paused to take this in.

'Yes, I know,' she said.

My heart sank. I joked with her to lighten my own mood, and
asked her to come with me to Guyana; I know full well that she is as
set against returning to Guyana as she is against ever stepping foot
in England again.

'Oh well,' she said, beginning to giggle. 'You must have drunk
creek water as a baby.' She was reminding me of the saying, *If you
eat labba and drink creek water, you will always go back to Guyana.*

Another of my cousins, now living in Canada, has brought his
daughter, in her thirties, for this mini-reunion, and he and his wife
are showing her the country for the first time. My cousins know this
country; they were older than I was when they left, and they have been
back regularly. They are able to say things like, 'Your grandfather
owned Dope Eyre's Tiny Cash Store on that road' and 'That's the
bank where your mother worked; the banks would only hire Chinese
and Portuguese people to work in them, no Indians or Blacks.'

These statements, delivered casually, prick me like tiny arrows.
My mother's skin is not fair, but in plantation classification, her
Chinese heritage made her acceptable. As a young girl I would watch
the effect of my mother's presence on family, friends and strangers.

'You must be sisters,' women in shops would say about her and my older sister. Men whistled at her in the street. I knew that she was beautiful inside and out, but I found no solace in that since neither of us were like the images of beauty in our North American life.

At the end of high school, I was restless and wanted out of the sub-urbs. I had become a sad seventeen-year-old. I knew that I wanted to be a writer, but it was not something I could discuss with my parents; it was not a profession in the way that they understood professions. I planned a back-packing adventure in Europe with a friend. Surely there I would be transformed into an artist like Joni Mitchell, a woman seeking herself, travelling the lonely roads of Greece and meeting men to give her back her smile.

We made vague plans, bought two railcards — one for travel in Britain and the other for western Europe — and arrived in London on a jet-lagged morning, where we fell asleep on a park bench near Victoria Station. We were woken by the cheers of a crowd and, to our astonishment, realised that the Queen was passing in a car.

England was mythical to us. We explored the main sights of London, visited York, the Lake District and Wales, as well as many other towns along the way. I carried a copy of Charlotte Brontë's *Jane Eyre* in my backpack. I identified with Jane's orphan status, despite the fact that I was part of a huge, close and connected extended family through my father's six siblings and my mother's three brothers, not to mention the legions of aunties, uncles and cousins from Guyana who were not blood relations. But an orphan is someone without a sense of continuity, and that was me — partly because of my confusion about *what* I was, but also inherent in the writer I was becoming. I identified with Jane's fiery will in the red room, her desire for independence and her insistence upon the truth. 'I am no bird,' she says, 'and no net ensnares me; I am a free human being with an independent will.'

And so was I.

I had little real knowledge of the English Romantic Poets, but in the Lake District I knew enough about the idea of a spontaneous overflow of powerful feelings to make the reality of walking where Wordsworth might have walked exhilarating. Jane was with me, falling in love with Rochester, and it became possible for me to believe that I too might find that soul mate who would one day say, '… it is as if I had a string somewhere under my left ribs, tightly and inextricably knotted to a similar string situated in the corresponding quarter of your little frame.'

Here at my cousin's house in Georgetown, after the kiss ka dee bird has flown off the shutter, I remember the moment when I read the passage in *Jane Eyre* that unhinged my fanciful link with its heroine. Jane describes for Rochester the ghost-like figure she has spotted roaming the corridors of Thornfield Hall. The figure is a woman, 'tall and large, with thick and dark hair hanging long down her back'. Her face is 'fearful and ghastly':

> '… oh, sir, I never saw a face like it! It was a
> discoloured face — it was a savage face. I wish I could
> forget the roll of the red eyes and the fearful blackened
> inflation of the lineaments!'

'Ghosts are usually pale, Jane.'

'This, sir, was purple: the lips were swelled and dark; the brow furrowed: the black eyebrows widely raised over the bloodshot eyes. Shall I tell you of what it reminded me?'

'You may.'

'Of the foul German spectre — the Vampyre.'

The description of Bertha Mason, Rochester's first wife, as purple, her lips engorged, her eyes bloodshot, was grotesque and yet familiar, the Gothic horror version of a woman. Self-loathing engulfed me, a shame whose source I did not yet fully understand.

In Innsbruck I met a twenty-five-year-old man who ran the backpacking hostel. Older and wiser, he was also handsome and accomplished — the perfectly educated European man I had envied if not exactly desired (I understand now that I wanted to *be* one of them rather than love one of them). He played Bach and Beethoven for us on the piano, and at the end of the night he and I were left alone in his room, the artist's studio of my dreams. We stood at the door reluctantly saying goodnight. He kissed me gently on the lips and then pulled back and gave my bottom lip the gentlest of bites, as though discovering something in it.

I was tantalised, and felt as if I had been let in to a sophisticated European courting ritual. This is what real men did. But now, as I sit in my cousin's house and the heat of the day builds, the veins on my arms stand out, my pores open and my body seems to swell into its proper fullness, I think he was probably just thrown off by the feel of my lips. I was not what backpackers to Innsbruck looked like in the late 1970s. I was exotic and strange. I look back now and am embarrassed that I thought I was just like all the other young women in the hostel, thinking maybe I'd go to Amsterdam or Rome, put flowers around my room and learn to play the piano.

As I walked through Georgetown yesterday, I thought again of Bertha Mason. At Thornfield Hall, Jane comes face to face with her own wild desire; the shock of seeing Bertha is the shock of a dark underside, perhaps of her own, perhaps the empire's, the dark mirror of the Victorian woman for whom the wealth of England was being built on plantations in the 'West Indies', among other outposts. Here in Guyana, I feel more like Jane than Bertha, because my wealth is conspicuous; my family abandoned this land to despots and corruption because we were privileged enough to be able to. Not all escapes are lucky, but ours was. And as I think of the plantation hierarchy, it's clear why.

Georgetown was prosperous in its days as the capital of the colony. Examining photographs of the main street in the 1880s and early 1890s, I think of Oxford or Bath, and of the ambition of Victorian architecture. Britain at the time favoured a range of architectural styles — Gothic, Tudor, Romanesque and Italian Renaissance. And yet I'm aware that the Georgetown buildings in these styles exist in a town that is below sea level. Homes in the capital were built on stilts to keep them above the encroaching sea. A series of trenches and walls were built to drain off flooding. In one photograph, the Law Courts building, finished in 1894, looks like a mashup of Shakespeare's Globe Theatre and an abbey in Rhineland. But it is built out of local timber, the greenheart tree that forms the skeleton of many of the buildings that still survive. In the photographs, the marble statue of Queen Victoria holds pride of place out front. Yesterday on my stroll, I noticed that although the building has been maintained and recently repainted, Victoria's arm and sceptre have been broken off, her nose is chipped and her throne is cracked and broken. My cousin told me that during the riots and suspension of the government in 1953 the statue's head was blown off with dynamite. In 1970, when Guyana became a cooperative Republic, the entire statue was removed. However, in 1990, the mayor restored and re-erected the statue, missing a limb and her symbol of imperial authority.

Law Courts, Georgetown, Guyana. Source: Photo by author.

In pre-independence Guyana, specific values underpinned everything: 'plantation society' governed all enterprises, and people were ranked and legitimised according to the values of the 'planter class'. Desire was for European riches; aspiration was for European achievements. Subcultures and subordinate groups were devalued. Professions, education and culture were modelled on British standards. People who had come from four different continents abandoned their original cultural identities. Food, music and language mixed, became like the 'cook-up rice' my grandmother used to make for us — a one-pot meal with ingredients from around the world. This 'creolisation' — in which people from different ethnicities are integrated into a predominant value system — caused the differences among the groups to be identified as 'racial', and the individuals within them to be placed in a hierarchy of social worth. Creole culture encourages social integration, but it also emphasises cultural differences and leaves room for some people to be excluded based on their ethnic backgrounds. It accounts for my mother being able to work at Barclays Bank, and for my Chinese grandmother warning me against marrying a black man.

The white population in British Guiana after slavery consisted of planters and estate personnel, colonial officials, professionals, merchants, priests and missionaries, soldiers and sailors. Significantly, they were never more than three per cent of the population, and they formed a kind of aristocracy. They were the main employers and patrons of the professions — lawyers, doctors, engineers — and they personified the immense dominance the plantation held over the society. This small percentage resonates with other small percentages in history and in the present — ownership in the hands of the few, profit valued over equality, a planter class recreated over and over and over again in different forms, with different products and different labourers.

The day before yesterday, on a trip to New Amsterdam on the Berbice River, close to the border with Suriname, my cousin mentioned casually that our Scottish great-great grandfather's cousins were overseers on a plantation in the district. Another tiny jolt had me imagining these relations with discomfort. I thought of the creolisation that made me, that created the complex racial mix and complex social circumstances of my entire extended family, and I became confused by feeling ashamed and proud at the same time.

Now as I sit at the window and the kiss ka dee bird returns, I think of my mother's lips, her beauty, and the history that is responsible for her, and I wish I had insisted that she come with me on this trip — my mother who loves her Caribbean heritage, her mixed background, and who has never been confused about 'what' she is.

Cicely Mavis McWatt (née Eyre). Source: Family photo.

There are women who pay a lot of money to cosmetically alter their lips so that they become as full as my mother's — so that they look more like Bertha Mason's than Jane Eyre's. The market for lip enhancement is estimated to be worth billions around the world. In the US, more than 29,000 lip-implant procedures took place in 2017, amounting to about one every 20 minutes.

And yet we don't normally describe these procedures as 'white women' becoming 'black women' in order to enhance their sex appeal. The cosmetics industry has detached the history of racialised bodies — the black slave who is deemed worthless by the plantation overseer or owner, dehumanised, raped — from products.

'Kiss ka dee,' says the bird.

'*Qui est là?*' says another.

> I heard the parrot call as he did when he saw a
> stranger, *Qui est là? Qui est là?* And the man who
> hated me was calling too, Bertha! Bertha! … Someone
> screamed and I thought, *Why did I scream?* I called
> 'Tia!' and jumped and woke.

This is Bertha Mason in *Wide Sargasso Sea*, foreshadowing her own death, in her own voice, which was given to her by Jean Rhys, who imagines Bertha's life before and after meeting Rochester and up to the moment of her desperate leap from the fire at Thornfield Hall. In *Wide Sargasso Sea* everything is inverted. The unnamed Rochester is a feeble, cowardly and ignoble version of Bronte's. Antoinette (Bertha's real name, given to her by Rhys) sees herself in the pool as her best friend, Tia. The parrot is constantly calling

'Who's there? Who's there?' I became obsessed with this white creole woman who in turn was obsessed with her black best friend, and I was sure that Jane Eyre had suppressed a part of her own dark psyche. The novel is a house of mirrors to Bronte's masterpiece and challenges it to be authentic and true to the darker side of what had happened in Rochester's life before Jane.

In the novel, I found compassion, not shame, for my Grandfather Eyre's story — for his time in the asylum like Bertha's in a locked attic — and I saw plantation dynamics with new insight. Antoinette Mason is disinherited from any status in society because she is poor. Her plight is a result of the collapse of the sugar trade in Dominica. Her poverty becomes her race, becomes her body. She is forced to marry for money. My middle-class body, connected to the 'Barclays bank ethos' of fair skin and employment, also became my race, giving me privilege and mobility.

When I am in this climate, my body responds to the air as though it is my own breeze; I am its bird, the kiss ka dee cousin. I have been back to the tropics regularly since that August as a child when my siblings and I measured our noses, unable to sleep from the anticipation of our holiday. In the tropical air I am in my body and I forget about my intellectual pursuits or my social context. As I walked through Georgetown, passing Quamina Street, a thoroughfare dedicated to the memory of the enslaved Akan man who was one of the leaders of the largest slave revolt in the British Colonies in 1823, I felt a timeless current running through the city. I realised how much I longed to see my father again. I wanted to turn back all the clocks and be here with him as a young man, to go with him to the dances, picnics at the sea wall, to see Mother Sally, the stilts dancer who dances her way through town ten feet high on Christmas morning. I missed him so much — even his last days of adjusting the plastic tubes that delivered his portable oxygen to his nostrils — that later that day, at Ogle airport, and just for a moment, I was sure he was here in Guyana.

We arrived for our flight to Mabaruma with only a backpack each; we would be staying a single night. Airport staff weighed us and our packs and sent us off to wait at the side of the room, while other passengers with heavier baggage were checked in with greater confusion and concern. A cage with some ducks, boxes of electrical appliances, sacks of grain: these were all coming with us.

On the floor to my left I noticed two tall white cylinders with something scrawled on them in black marker. Stepping closer, I realised the handwriting read, 'Dr McWatt, Mabaruma Hospital'. At first I thought it was my bad eyesight, but edging even closer I confirmed the words. My heart quickened. I alerted my companions, waving and pointing; these cylinders, which we assumed were full of oxygen, were intended for Dr McWatt in Mabaruma. My father was Dr McWatt and my cousin, whose eyes were now fixed on his name on a cylinder, is also a veterinarian like my father was. He and I shared a short, suspended moment trying to make sense of this. In my moment I imagined that I had misunderstood the physical realities of my father's corpse on the bed in the senior's home in Ontario, his oxygen detached; in fact, all he had needed was to get home. In Mabaruma he would be waiting for me, still elderly and in need of oxygen, to be sent regularly from Georgetown, but alive and enjoying the sea breeze, the perfumed air. My cousins didn't tease me when I told them about this magical thinking. Instead, as we flew over the rainforest towards Mabaruma, we agreed to try to find this Dr McWatt named on the cylinder.

Above: View from the Cessna airplane on flight from Georgetown to Mabaruma. Source: Photo by author.

Below: Oxygen Cylinder, Ogle Airport, Georgetown, Guyana. Source: Photo by author.

When we arrived, we kept our eyes peeled for who was there to pick up the cylinders, but all the cargo was carted off to be distributed later. On the way to our guesthouse, we passed the hospital and asked our taxi driver if he knew of a Dr McWatt, telling him that he might be a relative of ours. He looked at us curiously, then said quite boldly, 'He's a big black guy', as though no such connection was possible.

Later we dropped into the hospital itself and were told that the doctor was on leave that week, so I left a note for him, asking him to email me if he wanted to be in touch. We found out a bit more about him from Facebook, saw that he was, indeed, a very tall and imposing man in his thirties, who didn't look like anyone in the family. And he was from New Amsterdam, the same town where one of the original Scottish McWatts had been a plantation overseer.

We spent the day wandering through the tiny settlement, my cousin showing us where he'd walked the path to his one-room wooden schoolhouse, which was no longer standing; the house he'd lived in was now a bare, neglected wooden shell, peeling, and collapsing. We wandered through the riverside market alive with trade in fish, cassava, bananas, toiletries like 'crab' oil and coconut oil, some of which came in by river speedboats, and some on the corials — the dug-out canoes — of the indigenous people, along with huge sacks of flour being offloaded from a barge. The faces around us were a mix of so-called races: a blend of long and wide, fair and dark, the inhabitants of the Barima-Waini region, including Warrau and Arawak people.

My mind did circles on itself around the 'big black' McWatt and the faces of the indigenous people that looked like those of my sister and brother, like photos of myself as a child with two ponytails, resembling small coconut palm trees, on top of my head. But the differences between us were also clear. When the despots came, we had left. I now lived elsewhere.

A birthday party in Georgetown. I am just over two years old,
standing on the right in the second row in front of my sister.
Source: Family photo.

Three Scottish relatives arrived in British Guiana in the 1800s: two who were brothers, heading to New Amsterdam as overseers in the 1820s, to manage slaves, and their cousin, who was going west to Demerara. In documents related to slave complaints brought to criminal court in New Amsterdam in the 1820s, an overseer named McWatt is accused of provoking the attempted suicide of a slave who was forced into the stocks for being too drunk to perform his duties. The overseer was the elder cousin of my great-great grandfather.

The British National Archives lists this McWatt as a slave owner in 1822. In other documents concerning him, slaves complain of beatings, lashings, kicking. Later, the two New Amsterdam McWatt brothers ambushed the plantation manager and killed him. They were subsequently arrested, tried, found guilty of murder and hanged.

I am from the Demerara rather than the New Amsterdam branch of the family but the names link us, and the association with these other McWatt ancestors cannot be ignored.

I want to know more about the woman responsible for the browning of my branch of the McWatt family tree, but to speculate on who she was and what her circumstances were feels painful. Stories from historians and accounts from plantation owners themselves give me images of brutality at the heart of pre-abolition sexual relations. Those from post-abolition days might have been different. Or they might not have.

> Thursday, 30th January 1755: At night Cum Phibbah.
> Friday 31st: Nancy, Phibbah's sister, here tonight.
> Saturday, 1st February: About 2pm. Cum Phibbah.
> At night she slept in the cook-room. Sunday 2nd:
> Phibbah did not speak to me all day. Monday 3rd:
> About midnight last night I fetched Phibbah from her
> house. Had words with her again in the evening. At
> night Cum Phibbah. Friday 7th: Phibbah denied me.

These are the diary entries of Thomas Thistlewood, which he kept while serving as a plantation overseer and eventual slave owner on various estates in Jamaica between 1750 and 1786. A somewhat learned man, he uses Latin terms throughout the diary to detail more than 3,000 sexual 'conquests', which he recounts without shame: *cum* (with) to identify sexual intercourse; *sup. lect* (on the bed); *sup. terr* (on the ground); occasionally *in silva* (in the woods); *in mag* or *parv. dom* (in the great or small house); and, on less satisfactory occasions, *sed non bene* (but not well).

Most of his encounters were with the slaves he owned, one of whom — Phibbah — he had a life-long relationship with. He fathered at least one child that he claimed, known as 'Mulatto John'. While his accounts of rape are somewhat disguised by his prim Latin phrases, Thistlewood is also the man credited with inventing the 'Derby's Dose', a form of sadistic punishment of runaway slaves that involved rubbing salt, lime and pepper into open wounds while another slave defecated into the mouth of the runaway.

Even without the marriage records, or any specifics of the sexual relations in my family history, it's clear that African as well as Indian women were the purview of plantation overseers, and children arrived as a consequence.

I can make out faint tracks back to the parents of my great-grandfather — the one in the photo from the 1930s — but database entries on Ancestry.com fall short of reliable. According to the database, his Scottish father would have been sixty-one years old at the time of his birth, while his father's wife would have given birth to him at the unlikely age of sixty-two. The gaps in records create speculative stories, and they cause some people to disappear.

I'm certain stories of my African great-great grandmother have been passed down through her family, whoever they are, and

I imagine that with a different kind of research I could find out specific details. But whether or not she was a partner, lover, victim, confidante, employee or stranger to the man with whom she had a 'mulatto' (the word comes from the Portuguese word for 'mule' — *mulo* — and was intended to denote sterility, a clearly debunked hypothesis) child, she is absent from my history. She is Ralph Ellison's protagonist:

> I am invisible, understand, simply because people
> refuse to see me. Like the bodiless heads you see
> sometimes in circus sideshows, it is as though I have
> been surrounded by mirrors of hard, distorting
> glass. When they approach me they see only my
> surroundings, themselves or figments of their
> imagination — indeed, everything and anything
> except me.

It is my last day in Georgetown. I haven't heard from the Dr McWatt in Mabaruma, but I hope we will connect. As I fill out my immigration form at Ogle Airport, I put my middle name where my address should be. I scratch it out, but then worry about how messy it is and that it might appear misleading. I ask the immigration officer standing at the entrance to the departures gate if it's a problem. He looks at the form and asks me to redo it, and to put my destination address and my leaving address in the margin. I don't ask him why he requires this extra information for which there are no boxes. I do as he says. I show the form to him again, hoping he'll now let me pass through to immigration. He scans the form and looks up at me, examines my face and looks me up and down. Eventually he says, 'Are you from New Amsterdam?'

I think no one is going to believe me when I write this, but it is indeed happening. I hesitate, wondering if I should just shake my head, but I say, 'No. I live in London.'

'Oh,' he says.

'You know the McWatts?' I ask him.

'I went to school with one of them in New Amsterdam,' he says. 'Big guy!' And he waves his arm the way others have done when referring to the man whose name was on the oxygen cylinder.

'Yes, I think we're related,' I say.

He looks at me again, nods and opens the door to the immigration desk inside the terminal.

I arrive in Barbados where I'll spend a few days before returning to London. I stay in an apartment I rent regularly, on the south coast. Upon arrival I greet the woman who cleans here, and whom I recognise after many years. She and I exchange a few stories about how life in Barbados is now compared to the last time I was here. 'Hard, hard,' she says, 'the government is wotless.' I tell her that things seem to be getting better in Guyana, that there is talk of oil riches on the way and that Georgetown is more vibrant than the only other time I visited, so long ago. She is surprised to hear that I am Guyanese. I explain, and as I do I hear my accent change and a distinct Guyanese flavour emerge — the accent I must have had before I started to go to school in Canada. It surprises me, but I go with it, enjoy it, drawing out the vowels.

'You don't look like a Guyanese,' she says with a furrow in her brow. Then she smiles. 'You'ds look like a white lady.'

Later that day, I float on my back in the sea and gaze at the few clouds that drift above me. I imagine my great-great grandmother. We are together on a sugar estate in west Demerara, sitting in the shade of a coconut palm. She is cutting pineapple and offers me pieces as I ask questions. I eat ravenously and then grow tired of all my questions, my mind galloping with interconnections, with politics, with confusion, because we are deeply alike and yet so singularly distinct. She tells me stories that surprise me, stories that bore me too, which I can't seem to reconcile with my hunger for her. She tells me stories that make me feel like family and those that make me feel like a stranger. Tears come. She puts her hand on my forehead. I ask her for forgiveness. I think perhaps she laughs at me.

3

Eyes

This wondrous gift to her broke apart years ago, in China, but Grandmama kept the jade pendant in a tiny red silk envelope, and kept it always in her pocket, until her death.

When I arrive home in London, there is war.

Well, there is *more* war, or war *again*. The US, UK and France have dropped bombs on three chemical weapon sites in Syria, a country that has again attacked its own people.

There are different kinds of war in other places, right before me and inside me still, despite the April light, the magnolia blossoms, the aching readiness of green shoots just behind the pink blossoms of wild cherry trees. The fantasy I had of healing the past as I floated on my back in the Caribbean Sea is lost the moment I tune back into the news.

On the radio: Outcry against the BBC's decision to broadcast a live version of Enoch Powell's infamous 'Rivers of Blood' speech, read by an actor to mark the fiftieth anniversary of its delivery by the racist Member of Parliament who ranted about the 'dangerous' levels of immigration in the UK in the late 1960s. Why re-enact it? Why?

In the newspaper: Some of the 'Windrush Generation' — British citizens from the Caribbean who were invited to England to fill much needed gaps in the labour force between 1948 and 1971 — have lost their jobs, benefits and pensions, have been denied health care for terminal illness, have been asked to produce evidence of their legal status, have been sent to detention centres and even deported. One of them — it's important to say his name: Dexter Bristol — has died from heart failure attributed to stress from the trauma of being told he was in the UK illegally and fired from his job. Apologies have been made by the Home Secretary; reparations are being demanded, but the damage has been done. Racism thrives, social engineering is in progress and the plantation mentality that allows some citizens to be dispensable is alive and well.

On the internet: The shooter who opened fire on a Quebec mosque in 2017, killing six people, admits to his motives, saying 'I was watching TV and I learned that the Canadian government was going to take more refugees, you know, who couldn't go to the United States, and they were coming here … I saw that and I, like, lost my mind. I don't want us to become like Europe …'.

On social media: A placard in a protest against the bombing of Syria: 'If you don't want refugees, stop creating them.'

The wars I am tuning into have migration and displacement at their heart.

In a link from Twitter, I read the words 'epicanthic fold'. I click, follow and discover an article about a painter who has represented the progression of age in the 'Asian eye'. The epicanthic fold is the skin over the upper eyelid that covers the medial canthus — the corner where the upper and lower eyelids meet — of the eye. I examine the paintings carefully because I want to see what my eyes will look like in their old age, the extra folds, the wrinkles, the slow closing of the lids that I hope I live long enough to wear as my grandmother did. I think about the physiognomy of eyes in the making of race. The epicanthic fold is present in people from most parts of Asia, Polynesia and Micronesia, in indigenous Americans and indigenous people of the Nile Valley, and in Europeans. The folds are also apparent in children of any race, particularly before the nose bridge fully develops. Down's Syndrome, foetal alcohol syndrome and other conditions that cause the nasal bridge not to mature will also produce epicanthic folds. I meditate on the link between migration and immigration, between race and movement and epicanthic folds — another biologising of the body that is used to underscore difference. Difference in the blink of an eye.

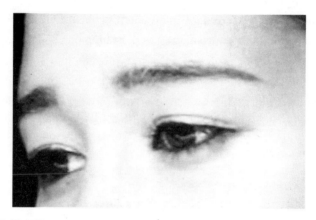

The epicanthic folds of my niece, Alanna McWatt. Source: Family photo.

The careful application letters my father wrote to the Canadian Immigration Department in the early 1960s were typed on thin, blue onion-skin paper, likely delivered by steamer rather than airmail, with a copy for his files which we discovered after his death.

In these letters, he outlines his professional training, his contacts, his hopes and his promised gratitude. These letters make me sad. My father was leaving all the things he had become as a man, leaving a job and a country he loved, for our future's sake, and was trying very hard to maintain his dignity. He was careful in his choice of words, and shows a hint of subservience that is difficult for me to digest.

The story of immigration in Canada is a complex one. Immigration to whose land? Whose country? Settler Europeans, First Nations, Inuk and Métis peoples still have land issues that are unresolved as I write. The disputes are the source of deep wounds in a country that is perceived from afar as one of the most harmonious, integrated and progressive in the world. But Canada is also a country with a history of colonialism, slavery, the cultural genocide of indigenous people through the residential school system, Japanese internment, the Chinese head tax, the War Measures Act and many of the same pitfalls of border-making that arise in any nation state.

At the heart of racism is the border.

And yet migration is part of what makes us human. From the movement of *Homo erectus* out of Africa across Eurasia almost two million years ago, through industrialisation, war, famine, partition, and to the current unfathomable refugee crisis around the world: we move therefore we are. And borders create the *us* and *them* that is the seed of war.

When I think of my parents' decision to leave British Guiana, I also think of my mother at her dead son's grave — how difficult it was for her to leave him in the rain. How difficult is it to leave the country of one's birth, the earth that covers one's buried ancestors and descendants, the potency of land and place and identity? Many people have no option, but because of my father's profession, he had three: Canada, the US or the UK. Had my father chosen the UK, I might have been among those of the Windrush generation without the appropriate paperwork, facing hostility from the Home Office, threatened with being deported 'home' even as a British citizen. My value and validity would now be negated. In contrast, my brother, sister and I were naturalised as Canadian citizens, by right of my father's application.

My father's first choice was Canada because he had been educated and trained there. As a boy he had tended his own goat, sheep and donkey in the backyard of his family home in Kitty. Life in the 1920s with six siblings was modest and he recounted tales of splitting one chicken for dinner among nine people, long trips in rattling carts on roads made of sun-dried mud and make-do games with discarded wheels. He got his first job in 1940 selling foodstuffs for five dollars a month. He saved and saved, was promoted, changed jobs and at last, in 1948, he had enough money to go on a schooner, the *Lady Nelson*, to study in Canada.

Errol McWatt, in his graduation photo from the University of Guelph, School of Veterinary Medicine. Source: Family photo.

After upgrading his qualifications in a high school, where he was humiliated by other pupils for being twenty-eight years old in grade twelve, he was accepted into the School of Veterinary Medicine at the University of Guelph. He didn't return home for the summer like most students, nor did he find career-enhancing jobs to support his studies. Instead he experienced the racism of small-town Ontario. He was denied a rented room in Guelph and had to resort to living and working on farms, picking asparagus in May and strawberries in June, with other odd jobs in July and August. When he graduated in 1952, he returned to British Guiana and eventually became District Veterinarian for an entire agricultural region. His dream job. He met and courted my mother; they married and began a family immediately, everything falling into place. Then came the tragedy of my brother's death. Because his hope for his other three children outshone any of his own aspirations for career or status, and because British Guiana's racial divisions were growing violent, he decided to make a move.

By the early 1960s, Canada had progressed from being a country in the shadow of both its neighbour to the south and its 'founding' island empire across the Atlantic, to become a burgeoning, productive country with a birth-rate that had almost doubled since 1940. At the time of my father's immigration application, the country had gone from seeing itself as a British (meaning white) society — an identity that left out indigenous people, French Canadians, and Black and Asian people — to a place that needed people like him in order to prosper.

It was no longer possible to maintain what was previously 'white' immigration, even though 'whiteness' had been enshrined in the 1910 Immigration Act, which had established the definition of an immigrant: northwest European immigrants were preferred. Had my father tried to immigrate as a student in the late 1940s, he would not have been successful. His European heritage would not have occurred to him or anyone else. I am quite certain that he never imagined his ancestor from Madeira holding squares of fishing-net like lace, and he would not and could not have claimed a right to immigration on the grounds of his Scottish heritage either. He would not have known that the 1910 Act laid out a plan for new immigration that in 1919 and 1923 was amended to include a policy of 'national origins' that clearly stated that Britain, the US, the Irish Free State, Australia, New Zealand and South Africa were preferred countries. The policy tried to ensure that any new comers to Canada ascribed to British values and, by extension, 'whiteness'. Those values were celebrated by 'Empire Day', a national holiday set up so that citizens could participate in organised displays of devotion to queen and country. But my father would have been familiar with this colonial hierarchy of values, though creolisation in Guyana had given his half-Chinese wife status in that society, whereas in Canada the Chinese had a very different immigration history.

In the late nineteenth century, Chinese labourers, who had mostly settled in British Columbia after being conscripted to do the dangerous and difficult work of clearing and grading and blasting through tunnels of rock to build the Canadian Pacific Railway, were considered undesirable Canadians, despite what they had contributed to the country's prosperity. According to the first Prime Minister of Canada, John A. Macdonald 'the Chinese has no British instincts or British feelings or aspirations'. He made it clear that the exclusion of Chinese migrants was necessary or 'the Aryan character of the future of British America should be destroyed'.

Along with the legislation, a 'white Canada' sentiment emerged in the early twentieth century, with a British Columbia premier declaring at a Conservative convention in 1909, in the face of growing Chinese immigration, 'We stand for a white British Columbia, a white land, and a white Empire.' The Chinese Head Tax — a fee that each Chinese person entering Canada was charged, in response to anti-immigration feelings in the late nineteenth century — was increased substantially after the turn of the new century, and that, along with the Chinese Exclusion Act of 1923, effectively put an end to Chinese immigration.

The Chinese Head Tax, the Coolie Bounty, the free movement of some but not others: immigration places differing values on some human lives. My father was a product of the 1860s plantation in Guyana that I have imagined, and as a result took random injustice for granted. He made his way through a system of economic stratification based on race, types of labour and proximity to whiteness that benefitted him in one colony and penalised him in another.

In 1947, the year before my father started his studies at Guelph, the Canadian prime minister, William Lyon MacKenzie King, made this point in the House of Commons:

I wish to make quite clear that Canada is perfectly
within her rights in selecting the persons whom
we regard as desirable future citizens. It is not a
'fundamental right' of any alien to enter Canada.
It is a privilege.

But fundamental human rights were exactly what were on the
table after the war, and they became the challenge to any immigration policy that discriminated on the basis of place of origin and
race. In the post-war world, scientific racism was scientifically
discredited, with UNESCO publishing their 'Statement on Race'
in 1950.

The biological fact of race and the myth of
'race' should be distinguished. For all practical
social purposes 'race' is not so much a biological
phenomenon as a social myth. The myth of 'race'
has created an enormous amount of human and
social damage.

But the structural inequality of the plantation is a difficult
pyramid to tear down.

Despite the growing openness of Canada in the late 1950s
and early 1960s, attitudes are much more difficult to change than
laws. Without taking indigenous people into account, the country
was trying to distinguish itself from its old-fashioned parents,
Britain — who were now much more interested in the European
Community than the Commonwealth. Indians, Bangladeshis,

Pakistanis, Sri Lankans, Indonesians, Filipinos — people of the newly independent nations of Asia after the war — called for an end to Canada's racially based immigration policies. In Quebec, the Quiet Revolution, a time of economic and social development for French Canadians, was taking hold and Englishness was being cast off. If Canada wanted to stay together as a nation it would have to retreat from its purely English identity. And if it wanted to progress economically, it would need a workforce to help it do so.

In 1962, the year my family went to Canada, new immigration legislation was passed that eliminated quotas or restrictions based on nationality or geography or regions of the world, which meant that race had been written out of policy and replaced with a skills-based assessment. On paper, this was a huge structural change, but in practice and in public conversations, even the government admitted that, 'We prefer our immigrants from our traditional sources ... and while we are bound by the provisions of the new Immigration Regulations to service applications anywhere in the world, there is nothing to prevent us from concentrating our promotion of immigration from our traditional sources.'[1]

Nevertheless, my family was in.

And we worked hard to fulfil the promises my father made in his letters of application. My sister gravitated towards the law, my brother towards medicine, and I read and read and read in order to find myself, a self that was spread throughout a range of literature from people of many different backgrounds.

I discovered writers like Dionne Brand and Austin Clarke, who wrote about a 'there' and a 'here' of the Caribbean and Canada that I identified with, a blackness that I felt. Later, I encountered writers such as American Jenny Zhang and Canadian Wayson Choy who articulated for me the kind of inside-self/outside-self of an outsider that I associate with the Chinese heritage of my grandmother.

Jenny Zhang's *Sour Heart* is a book of unbelonging I wish had been available to me as a young person. The stories are unapologetic, visceral, they make poverty disgusting, they are funny and obscene — all the things I wanted to be able to write about in my twenties but had no models for. At the centre of the stories are young Chinese female narrators who navigate sorrow and love like toy boats on weedy ponds. They are lucid and frank about being immigrants who are not 'good'. They are ruthlessly themselves, yet still feel the pressure of ancestry, the desire to be worthy of their parents' sacrifices. This is the weight that my sister, brother and I also bore. To be good enough, and not to allow our intense 'inside' lives as strange brown people in the suburbs to tarnish the perfect 'outside' selves we were striving to achieve based on a belief in freedom and the promise of a 'fresh start' that is the myth of the North American dream.

Freedom is a confusing dream. It is both seductive and yet not fully understood by those of us who strive for it. What does it mean to be free in Europe or North America? Free from what and whom? The quest for freedom is one of the profound inheritances of my education, steeped in Enlightenment thinking and values. I felt it in my post-hippie dreams in Toronto and read about it in the books that extolled its existence in a world no longer bound by traditional religions. That thinking holds reason, progress and liberty as crucial to a civilised life on earth. It is a key part of all that I've learned to be as a North American, and yet paradoxically it is also an ideology from the eighteenth century that created a hierarchy of human civilisations. Philosophers like Immanuel Kant claimed that 'Humanity exists in its greatest perfection in the white race ... the yellow Indians have a smaller amount of Talent. The Negroes are lower and the lowest are a part of the American peoples.'[2] This is plantation mentality 101. And it trapped me into striving to be that good immigrant (in Canada and in the UK), that perfect self that will never be achieved — the desire for the toy-poodle instead of the mutt that our family ended up with, and that I am. And it also aligned my achievements with race, as a way of demonstrating how much I have 'overcome.'

Part of me has longed for a profound connection to a single tradition, one ethnicity or culture or territory to fully inhabit. I long for a simple past, in which individuals are not free in the modern sense, but in which a traditional community makes demands on its members simply by the fact of being born into it. I have been nostalgic for a relationship with the eastern traditions of my grandmother that I never had — that she never had, having been born in British Guiana. Still, she insisted on cooking Chinese food and on visiting Chinatown every week after we moved to Toronto. Tiny objects — the porcelain doll, the Chinese fan, the engraved jewellery box that she kept on the table beside her bed — were dear to her. I long for a tradition in which my grandmother is not running, has not been hurt and occupies a place of status in her society because she is an elder.

In Wayson Choy's *The Jade Peony*, a young boy, Sek-Lung, lives in the glow of his grandmother, Poh-Poh, who infects him with the gift of secrets between them. He engages in her mystery through fantasy, play and the ancestral tradition of fashioning windchimes from 'splendid junk':

> There, in the midst of her antique shawls, the old
> ancestral calligraphy and multi-colored embroidered
> hangings, beneath the mysterious shelves of sweet
> herbs and bitter potions, we would continue doing
> what we had started that morning: the elaborate
> windchime for her death … 'It will sing and dance
> and glitter,' her long fingers stretched into the air,
> pantomiming the waving motion of her ghost chimes;
> 'My spirit will hear its sounds and see its light and
> return to this house and say goodbye to you.'

I lived similarly in my grandmother's glow, watching her perform her imitation of Charlie Chaplin's walk to make me laugh, as I waited for the chow mein that was steaming on the stove. She was 'eastern' to me, with secrets and mystery in her tiny frame.

My DNA seems apparent to some people and not others. In the playground as a child I listened to other children make jokes about Chinese people, which didn't seem to include me, or I didn't notice if they did. I heard about the 'slanty-eyed chink', 'chink food', and Dr Fu Manchu. A teenage boyfriend affectionately called me a 'slope'. My Barbadian auntie called me Suzie Wong as an endearment, to differentiate me from my siblings and members of her own family, naming a kind of exotic grace she thought I possessed. It was a nickname that stuck for many years. It was only much later in my life that I learned that the Suzie everyone was referring to, from the movie *The World of Suzie Wong*, was a prostitute.

My grandmother's relationship to Chinese tradition was disrupted by her family's move to British Guiana, but because of our closeness, it is the only single tradition that I have ever imagined I could fully inhabit. It is the tradition that as a child I imagined might be truly mine, and yet for some reason I have not yet travelled to China.

I telephone my mother, who is lucid today and chatty. I ask about something else she once told me, long after the story of my grandmother's rape, possibly when I was in my twenties, when I was full of questions about her life, my grandmother's life, her friends' lives — everything I could get from her about what it was like to be women of their generations. She described her own maternal grandfather as a short man with a thin-tendrilled moustache and a Confucius beard, who would visit her in Georgetown from the countryside. He would bring fruit and small gifts for her and her brothers, and he had a giggle that I imagine was much like hers and mine. She tells me again that her grandparents lived far away from Georgetown and only her grandfather ever visited. She never met her grandmother. When I ask her to confirm what she told me as a young woman, she does not hesitate. She remembers that her grandmother had bound feet.

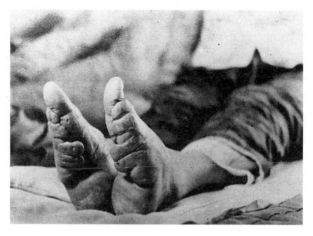

Feet which have been bound, binding removed.
Source: Wellcome Collection CC BY.

A woman only three generations removed from me. I imagine my great-grandmother at nine years old. She sits on a small stool in her village in southern China. It is the third year she has been forced to sit still while long cloth bandages are wrapped around her right foot, then her left. The first year, the bandages were wound in a figure eight from the heel across the instep and over the toes, then back, over and over again, drawn as tightly as possible. Her legs became inflamed from the lack of circulation, a few bones were broken in her foot. In the second year, the new bandages wrapped the back of the heel, forcing the foot towards the ball. Her feet buckled, and a few more bones broke above the arches. At nine, her feet are wrapped again to narrow them, and she is forced to stand and walk back and forth in the small room on her poor aching feet. The binding ritual will continue for two more years, until her ball and heel are so close together she can tuck a half-crown piece in the space between them. Only then is the foot said to be bound. She doesn't know that the foot binding is meant to bring her an advantageous marriage, her tiny feet fitting a girl only for a life of idleness, to be displayed as a symbol of wealth and status.

My great-grandmother, a peasant, married the sweet man with the Confucius beard and escaped China during war with the Japanese to start a farm and a small shop in the countryside of Demerara. She had lotus feet, but no status whatsoever.

Tradition or freedom? Nothing in my lineage is free, except an idea that has come through Enlightenment philosophers who are white, male and European. Their idea of freedom comes by way of ignoring the freedom or bondage of others, with collateral damage and roadblocks. And the tradition I long for comes with bound feet.

At this crossroad where I find myself — my mother's *Oh, the world* — on edge and uneasy in discussions about identity, when war is in the air and on the airwaves, what is our path? History demonstrates that there are always new paths.

In my twenties, my grandmother went to live with my mother's brother and his family in Ottawa because my parents had bought a farm in rural Ontario. When she moved, it felt like the heart of my family had been torn away from me, even though I was living my own life by then. I asked my mother for more and more stories about her life and my grandmother's because my reading had become focussed on feminist literature. The fact that I had been racialised in many ways up to this point in my life didn't stop me from believing that the overarching problem in the world was the patriarchy and that once the dream of feminism was realised, we would all have equality.

Toronto was becoming multicultural, and while attitudes were taking time to catch up with legislation, multiculturalism was an official policy in the country. I was involved in the feminist community through *Fireweed Quarterly*, and I took my new politics home, alienating my family, who were hesitant about 'radical' viewpoints; I was still the outsider telling stories to George the monkey. But now George the monkey was the blank page of notebooks in which I wrote poems and stories, the very first of which was published in *Fireweed*.

Around this time, race re-emerged as a prominent dividing issue. In 1983, *Fireweed* editor Makeda Silvera made a powerful speech to the Women and Words Conference in Toronto criticising white feminism for excluding black women and women of colour; in 1987 the Women's Press was in disarray and had a very public split over voice appropriation and racism; and in 1989 white author and feminist June Callwood and black author and feminist NourbeSe Philip argued publicly over the lack of representation of writers of colour in Canadian PEN.

At a Women's Day March that year, I was with two friends somewhere in the depths of a long, snaking pack of women carrying banners, chanting different versions of *hey hey, ho ho* and feeling emboldened and optimistic on a sunny spring day. A few minutes into the march, one of the organisers approached me from the side-lines and asked me to move to the front of the march.

I did that same fazed blinking I must have done when my teacher asked me 'What are you?'

'We are asking women of colour to walk at the front of the march this year,' she said.

I looked at my friends, who seemed as surprised as I was, but I understood what she was asking and didn't know what to do. I asked if I could bring my friends with me. The woman suggested that might defeat the purpose. And so I followed her closer to the front, towards the 'colour line' as I saw it, me straddling it, marked by duality, but feeling like I'd done the right thing in making myself visible in the march.

It was the moment I became politically black. I saw more clearly the fallacy of the grassy knoll in which we had already become 'one', and yet I was unable to speak to the kinds of racist attacks and the exclusion that most black women had faced. I became aware of 'whiteness' — my own and that of many of my white friends — as a state of mind that allows erasure and violence towards others while claiming liberation for all. It was another moment of shame, when difficult, uncomfortable knowledge rushed in. I felt like a fraud, unentitled to walk at the front of the march. Not black enough.

Not anything, but a lot of things. In Puerto Escondido I have been spoken to in Spanish, mistaken for a fellow Mexican. In Jamaica I have been asked which part of Kingston I am from. In the Dominican Republic I have been asked for directions. In Kenya I was told by a Maasai man that I could be his sister, not because of the colour of my skin but because of my eyes. In Paris I met the person who took the photograph of the man standing in front of the tank in Tiananmen Square. He looked deeply into my face and told me that my ancestors came from Guangdong. Last year on a flight to Gran Canaria, a man asked me in Spanish whether I wasn't always proud to be returning home to our land every time I flew above it.

Something about the shape of eyes, perhaps — while we all read one another for kinship — tells us that we belong to one another. But how can such a profound desire be satisfied through body parts?

In his last interview before his death in 2017, John Berger said, 'I think that all desire, including sexual, is the desire to be in a certain place, if only a place consoles us and gives us energy. But when I say place, I don't mean a geographical place … It's where your finger fits or where your foot rests, turned outwards.'

Where does my finger fit? My foot rest?

In my imagination and my desire for connection I tell myself stories in which I come from everywhere, sharing the same eye folds as people from all parts of the world. Theories about how the first inhabitants arrived in what is now known as the Americas continue to be proposed and contested: from the long-held belief that pre-historic humans crossed the land mass known as the Bering Land Bridge as early as 30,000 years ago, to other theories about multiple migrations by boat. All theories are speculative, with sparse evidence, weak dating methods and subjective interpretations. But, whether through forced transplantation or migration, I am a product of east and west, north and south. These stories relieve me of the pain of belonging nowhere and give me the key to everywhere. As I once longed for a singular place, a singular ethnicity or plot of land over generations, I now long for its opposite, for a space beyond belonging. I have travelled to many places in order to scope a sense of ownership or repatriation, but as I try to square my politics with my privilege, it seems that my only true inheritance is that I am always running somewhere else.

Two decades after that pivotal Women's Day March in Toronto, I flew to Cambodia on the recommendation of a friend who felt it was a safe place for women to travel alone. I wanted to write something about the Asia I was connected to, and to find another place where my *foot might rest*.

In Phnom Penh I don't particularly stand out — perhaps people see something in my eyes that they recognise — but my clothing is all wrong. I buy light cotton shifts and silk tops, becoming the colours of the environment: fuchsia, saffron and multitudes of green. I hold my breath as I walk the streets, against the smell of rotting fish and garbage, the waft of sewage from the river where blue and orange plastic bags float like lotus flowers. A big business development along the Sisowath quay blocks any wider view of the Mekong River.

To give my journey a bigger purpose, I have made contact with the programme manager of an NGO and plan to write about volunteering and the networks that support it. I think volunteering must be the wrong word for it. I'm looking for mechanisms that marry wealth and poverty. I'm looking to write about what happiness is — my own? yours? — if it exists while there is poverty.

I've brought John Berger's book *Hold Everything Dear* with me.

In it he warns against the 'devilish temptation of thinking that any struggle is over', and I take that to heart as I seek out how to feel comfortable in the world.

I travel by boat, along the Mekong River and then across Tonlé Sap Lake. More blue plastic, more orange, now yellow, now white plastic bags. Shacks on stilts, whole neighbourhoods on stilts like spider legs embedded below the water. Dug-out fishing boats putter up and down the lake, among the shacks. The floating villages are communities of Vietnamese and Cambodians who harvest the fertile lake and provide the country with most of its freshwater fish. Young children out with their parents, steering and pulling up nets, catch a country's dinner. One of the boats pulls alongside ours and our engine cuts; we drift, as I watch the driver of our boat exchange a tin of cooking oil for a bucket of fish. Simple and basic — the kind of exchange I'm seeking.

But nothing is as simple as it first appears.

I arrive in Siem Reap. It has been many decades since teachers, artists, intellectuals and anyone opposing the genocidal Pol Pot agrarian revolution were either killed or chased away. As I travel by tuk tuk into town, I notice a distinct lack of grey-haired people my parents' age. The town seems to be thriving, but something unhinged thrums beneath it; peace seems impossible in light of the country's history. I attribute the thrum to money — to Cambodians urgent to catch up with the rest of booming Asia, competing for tourists and investment. There's no time to look back and consider where all the grey hair went.

I tend to look back. But here I do not feel like a stranger. The programme manager of the volunteer organisation I've connected with tells me stories, and so do school children, tuk tuk drivers, bus boys in restaurants, all wanting to practise their English. I wonder if it might be possible for me to migrate away from so-called progress, to live here and still be myself in a society that doesn't have individual freedom at the centre of its values.

I travel to the temples of Angkor Wat. Walking past the temples, ruined walls and buttresses, I am in awe of the scale and the craftsmanship, but all I can think of in this heat is that people had to sit here and carve, for hours on end. What were the conditions like for those who built this? The hands of the men who carried these stones? Their backs? I think again of sugar. There are so many ways to conquer people.

I come to a crumbling temple with a tree pushing up through it. The tree, hundreds of years old, clings to the exposed earth between the stones that were laid in the twelfth century, offering the ruins protective shade to slow their decay. I marvel at how earth and buildings, destruction and growth, can co-exist.

On the way back to my bed and breakfast, my tuk tuk driver tells me that when he first saw me he thought I was Korean, the new kind of Korean woman who seems to be travelling a lot to Cambodia to spend money. He apologises when I tell him I live in London, and insists that there is a place I must see. I agree to let him take me to it.

At the floating village, he points to an entrance where another man will greet me. I transfer from tuk tuk to boat and am on the lake again. Vietnamese girls no more than six or seven years old paddle up to us, trying to get my attention. I turn and see that they are holding up the heads of large pythons, who are wrapped around their necks like scarves. The girls want me to touch the pythons. I freeze. The boatman tells me it will be fun. I scream inside. He translates what the girls say, suggesting that I visit their crocodile farm, which floats in the river just a few yards away, in the pit of a boat that also has souvenirs for sale. I beg the boatman to take me back to shore, and when I am dropped off implore my tuk tuk driver to hurry up and get going. We are silent all the way back to my B&B.

I feel lonely.

I leave Siem Reap and head south, towards the sea.

The friend who suggested I travel to Cambodia has given me a birthday gift — a stay in a Corbusier-styled designer residence, with eleven exclusive rooms, inhabited, I find out, by Belgians, British and a few Germans. When I arrive, I'm overwhelmed with shame at the luxury of it all. I feel unworthy. But I am tired, hungry and grateful for the peace, the silence. As I recline on a canopy bed that looks out over the sea, I read John Berger. He reminds me that poor people live with wind, dampness, flying dust and unbearable noise, with ants, with large animals, with smells, rats, rain, rumours and each other. I watch the sea. I close my eyes in the silence.

The next day, I meet a Frenchman who takes me in a jeep to Bokor Mountain, the highest peak in the Elephant Mountain range. We head to a dilapidated hill station that once could be reached only by elephant and was a lavish summer playground for the king and his colonialist friends.

The jeep lumbers up through clouds and into the clearing at the peak. The view is breathtaking, the air cool. The Frenchman tells me that after Independence in 1953, some of the highest rollers and biggest losers at roulette and cards in the casino, inconsolable, hurled themselves from the parapet. The jungle below has been fertilised by the uncounted dead: Pol Pot's victims who were bull-dozed over the cliff, mutilated and dumped into the jungle; convicts and coolies who perished building the original road. Later, the casualties from the Vietnamese invasion that ended the regime were also tossed here. I hold on to my perch. I think I see dead people. Everything is unsettling.

We watch an enormous, graceful eagle sweep out of its nest in the canopy and glide away.

Over the next few days I pursue oblivion to distract myself from the unsettling feeling.

I sail in a small dinghy.

I get a massage from a woman on the beach who is sure I must be Thai.

I eat *crabe au poivre* made with the finest Kampot pepper.

I kiss the Frenchman under a lopsided moon and the giddy stars surrounding Orion's belt.

The next day, sprawled out on the canopy bed again, I carry on with reading Berger: 'Many people have lost all their political bearings. Mapless, they do not know where they are heading ...'

A Belgian woman comes in from her boat ride and strides over to me, announcing that she's here, she's sorry she's late, but she's ready for her massage. I look at her with that now familiar blinking stare, wondering what to say. She speaks louder, as though I haven't heard or understood. She tries English, reminds me that she's booked in for two o'clock, and begins to take off her clothes. She lies down beside me.

I am struck dumb, and am not pretending when it appears I speak neither French nor English. My heart races, a burning feeling growing in my throat. I flee, disappearing to the roof to hide.

On the roof, the next passage I read by Berger is on madness. He writes that madness is found in the binary opposition of fear and confidence, when there is no negotiation between the two; for example when there's nothing to do but 'buy' or 'sell', no way to make gold out of grey-haired ancestors. As Primo Levi, who survived Auschwitz, said, 'You feel others have died in your place, that we're alive because of a privilege we haven't deserved, because of an injustice done to the dead. It isn't wrong to be alive, but we feel it is.'

On my last night in luxury I retreat to the rooftop again to stare out at the sea. The sun is going down in front of me just as the full moon rises behind me. The beauty is too much. It's beauty that requires you to live.

I stare out over the sea. It's like being on a ship at night, and there's that privileged silence again. *Hechoo, hechoo* ... the gecko chants below me. Laughing at me.

I don't blame it.

I am only a chameleon in the moonlight.

I fall asleep under its glow, on the roof.

There is no singular place I can belong. There is no shame in that. No shame.

4

Hair

The master had said, 'You are ugly people.'
They had looked about themselves and saw
nothing to contradict the statement; saw,
in fact, support for it leaning at them from
every billboard, every movie, every glance.
'Yes,' they had said. 'You are right.'

In 1850, at the third meeting of the American Association for the Advancement of Science, in Philadelphia, Peter A. Browne presented a study of human hair, exhibiting the world's largest collection of hair and launching his book, *The Classification of Mankind, By the Hair and Wool of Their Heads*. Blacks with their 'wool' and whites with their 'hair' belonged to different species, he told the assembled scientists and general public. His and other similar proclamations at the time created an enduring attitude toward African hair that would eventually lead to the quest for alchemy that would change 'wool' to hair, breeding loathing, self-loathing and industries of hair that fuel a beauty economy. But hair and wool are chemically indistinguishable, both made of keratin. The only real distinction between them is how the words are used: sheep are said to have wool, while humans have hair. The body. Race. A bad story.

It's a sunny day in late May in London, my father's birthday — he would have been ninety-six. Returning home from the Turkish grocery with some fresh garlic, Italian parsley and olive oil for the pasta dinner I'm making for a friend, I stroll dreamily along the pavement of a street in my neighbourhood in northwest London. The Victorian terraced houses look friendlier in May than they do in November, and even though there is rubbish strewn on the pavement and overflowing from bins, I am buoyed by springtime optimism. The trees are fully clothed again, recovered from the shame of winter — dressed in shades of green that defy my vocabulary for them. The plane trees surprise me most. Cut back early every year, they are reborn each May, with bouquets of clustered leaves — Parakeet green? Shamrock green? — that sprout from the thick trunks and branches. They are trees that need to be tamed each year in order to perform their summer duties.

The air is soft, humid, the kind of air that makes my skin feel cared for — similar to the air into which I was born. In this gentle humidity my hair gets bigger, fatter — with a bit more curl. It is wavy and fine, but I have a lot of it, and it's fuller in this air than in dry weather, and I feel more as I was born to be.

I walk past a house where a young builder is taking a sledge-hammer to some bricks that form a low wall. He stares at me as he raises the hammer. He shakes his head and sighs as I pass, so loudly that I turn round to look him in the eye, genuinely wondering if something is wrong with him and if I can help. He mouths some words, and my heart stops. I'm not sure but I think the words were 'black' and 'bitch'. I hurry down the street away from him. This kind of targeting is a first for me.

A South-Asian Canadian friend who has lived in London for nearly thirty years was accosted in the street in the days following the Brexit vote in 2016 and told that he should 'go home'. His incident and mine are mild compared to what others have experienced: a Muslim woman was dragged along the pavement by her hijab; two Polish men were attacked and one of them killed by six teenagers; a Muslim man and woman were squirted with acid, leaving them with life-changing injuries. Police figures show that in some areas of Britain in the eleven months after the EU referendum hate crimes rose as much as fifty per cent.

I want to be wrong about what I heard. It has been only three days since the wedding of Meghan Markle to Prince Harry — an event featuring an African-American preacher and black gospel music — and I wonder about what is in the air, for the young builder, for the country. There have been articles in the newspapers with headlines like, 'Can Meghan Save the Kingdom?'; 'Meghan Markle, Feminist Princess'; and 'How Meghan Markle Broke the Mould to Create Brand New Fairy Tale'. Everywhere there is talk of how the marriage is moving the monarchy forward — how it demonstrates the new, non-racist Britain.

But all I can see is the wealth of the plantation house Markle has entered.

Markle, like that other icon of progress, Michelle Obama, have 'relaxed' or straightened hair. In Victorian England, a woman's hair was the emblem of her beauty and femininity. Hair was long and very rarely cut. Even though in public it was worn up or in a chignon, in private women took pride in letting it down to its glorious length.

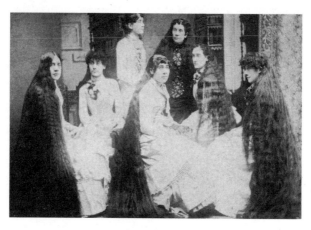

1880s Seven Sutherland Sisters singing group.
Source: H. Armstrong Roberts / ClassicStock / Getty Images.

In the plantation house, the governing aesthetic would have been for straighter hair, not 'wool'. The mixed-race children of slave masters, whose looser curls brought them closer to a white inheritance, often became the house slaves, spared the gruelling fieldwork of the plantation.

In communities of women of colour, hair is aspirational, a topic of debate, competition, ancestry, appropriation, decolonisation and a totem of racial consciousness. For some, 'good' hair is white hair.

Body consciousness, the pushback against body shaming and the fight for the so-called freedom to be any kind of woman we want to be are all movements that aim to rid women of pressure to be something they aren't. Pressure related to hair is similar to pressure related to weight and other markers of 'beauty'. I don't accept the word 'relaxed' for the chemical warfare and assault on the body that goes into straightening tight, wiry curls. Chemical products used to 'relax' hair break the hair's disulphide bonds — the strongest, naturally occurring bonds in nature. The protein structures of a hair shaft are held together by these bonds and hydrogen bonds — the ones that are easily broken by wetting them with water. Destroying the elasticity and strength of the disulphide bond by perming or relaxing the hair changes its shape. The chemicals used — sodium hydroxide or calcium hydroxide and guanidine carbonate — can burn the scalp and cause hair to fall out in handfuls.

The Brazilian Blowout is a professional smoothing solution used with a flat iron to make hair glossy, frizz-free and straight for up to twelve weeks. This treatment is controversial for a number of reasons, one of which is that the solution contains formaldehyde, which is a complex compound used in disinfectants, photographic processing and in embalming the dead — the ultimate in relaxation.

Women are not the only ones who fall prey to insecurity and shame about their hair. Malcolm X, in his autobiography, reflects on his 'first really big step toward self-degradation: when I endured all of that pain, literally burning my flesh to have it look like a white man's hair'. The Black Power of the 1960s and 1970s, made natural hair a symbol of freedom and expression.

In the long summer of 1970, while we measured noses for fun

and waited with excitement to take that first trip to Barbados, my sister, brother and I killed time watching endless hours of television in our suburban basement. A Wanted poster of Angela Davis often appeared in the news breaks between *The Flintstones* and *The Beverly Hillbillies*. Davis became a fugitive after a warrant for her arrest charged that she supplied the weapons used by a young African-American man in a courtroom shooting that resulted in the death of a judge. Her full afro overwhelmed her facial features. The only other hair we'd seen like that was on the actor who played Linc in the *Mod Squad*, a favourite show. To me, natural hair and black power is still linked to Angela Davis.

FBI Poster of Communist activist Angela Davis.
Source: Bettmann / Contributor / Getty Images.

Markle and Obama represent for me a confusion of power and blackness, in that their dress, their hair, are closer to codes of whiteness than blackness. Their position in the 'master's house' appears like 'success' in that they have joined the elite. Their aspiration, success and acceptance seem like a model path towards 'freedom' from the labour of the field.

As a toddler in Guyana, I had straight, thin hair. As a young girl in elementary school in Canada, I became aware that long hair was what real girls had, so I refused to allow mine to be cut, growing it eventually to my waist. My hair became thicker as I grew up, with odd curls and waves in random places, which I took care to brush out. In the 1970s, long hair was a reaction to the beauty parlour 'dos and perms of women in the generation before us. It was associated with a rebellious youth culture and hippie hair, which even young girls like me were influenced by. But there is something persistent in long, flowing locks defining femininity, and I succumbed to it.

A lady with hair reaching down to her feet.
Source: Hulton Collection / Getty Images.

My mother also has straight hair, but she has permed it since she was a young woman. I asked her recently why the perm, and she told me she didn't like her straight hair because it was too fine and lifeless. Her mother had complained about the curls, but my mother was adamant about them. 'Charlie had beautiful thick straight hair,' she said about my deceased brother. The sudden shift in focus to her lost first child surprised me, but I am noticing that her grief has been surfacing more often recently, as other memories subside, and topics to do with the body spark clarity. The tighter and tighter curls — towards an afro — that my mother had later in her life I now see as a reversal of her plantation privilege that allowed her to work at Barclays Bank in Georgetown.

By the time I was ten years old, my long hair felt too conspicuous. I asked my mother to take me to the salon and begged the reluctant stylist for short hair. I cried all the way through the session, sitting in the chair, watching in the mirror as my identity floated away from my shoulders and splayed out on the floor around me. With my hair in a pixie cut, my face felt too big, too ugly, too exposed.

I grew my hair back, but never as long, appreciating the freedom that shorter hair allowed me. I felt stronger and faster without it — a reversal of the Samson myth. I was catcher on the softball team, captain of the volleyball team, and I could outrun many girls on the track. Boyish, fast, I was fulfilling something for my parents.

Stepping up to bat in Willowdale. Source: Family photo.

When I was fifteen years old, I was a competitor in the Toronto Track and Field Finals. Decades later, I heard a story from one of my closest friends who was also there, though we hadn't yet met. At the end of a long day of competition, when most of the other events had wrapped up and the medals awarded, she heard a buzz at the far end of the track, at the high jump pit. As a fellow athlete ran past, she asked him what was going on. 'Some girl's breaking all the records,' he said, and she also ran after him to see. She found a girl with long, strong legs and a wiry body focussed on the high jump bar in front of her. The other jumpers had crashed out many inches before, and now she was competing against herself, having already broken last year's record. The jumper's eyes were fixed on the bar, and she seemed unaware of the crowd growing around her. She measured out the required steps from the bar and took her time to visualise her approach in a J that would land her left foot at the perfect spot in front of the bar to propel her body up. And then her arm would lead her body in a twist onto her back, allowing her head, shoulders, torso and finally — with a kick at the end — her legs to rise up in the air. She started her approach. Her Fosbury flop was perfect and she cleared the bar. The small crowd cheered. The officials raised the bar another half an inch. She cleared it again. Twice more, she undertook the same ritual, breaking a record each time, until finally the height defeated her.

I was the jumper, aiming higher and higher. Now I see it as a metaphor for my aspiration: to fit in, to do better, to be not only enough but the best. I see how much I struggled to be accepted. Winning, sailing over the bar, felt like freedom, like success. Achievement in sport is acceptable black attainment. Sport is a space in which black people have been allowed to achieve success. Dance, sing, run, sista.

I remember that on that day, I was 'in the zone' — the way all athletes describe these moments when they transcend what they perceive as their physical limitations. I enjoyed myself in that moment, but I wonder about the force of my determination. I feel how it was linked to wanting the toy-poodle puppy my white neighbours had. I understand aspiration.

Women contort, torture, butcher our own bodies in order to belong, to succeed, to find power in the plantation structure. A study conducted by the Perception Institute in 2016, called the 'Good Hair' Study, measured respondents' unconscious bias against black women's hair, with results suggesting that people associated the notion of 'pleasant' more often with smooth hairstyles than textured hairstyles. It also suggested that black women had more anxiety surrounding hair issues than white women and felt more pressure to straighten their hair for work — sometimes pressure from their employers. While the study indicates that things are changing drastically with younger women, a majority of people, and particularly white women, had some bias against black women based on their hair. This bias feeds shame and the industries that offer solutions. The black hair industry is said to be worth tens of billions. For the extensions it offers, it harvests real hair from Indian women who are poorly paid for their shiny straight locks. The hair is black in colour but not African in texture. Good hair is Indian too.

Being part of an elite might feel like freedom, might feel like jumping and sailing over a bar. But at the heart of power, it doesn't matter if your hair is an Angela Davis afro or the relaxed hair of a duchess. The plantation mentality can accommodate black owners, black leaders, as long as that power is maintained. Whiteness is a state of mind that encourages inequality.

———

To support myself while developing as a writer, I secured a job as an acquisitions editor for an educational publisher in Toronto. After three years learning about editing and the book process, enjoying the social life and making dear friends, I found myself not only as fragmented as I'd felt for most of my life, but shattered inside, trying to be someone I wasn't — cut off from my creativity. Neither the achievement nor the financial stability in an office job would bring me the kind of freedom I sought.

Pantyhose became the symbol of my discontent. They were a crucial part of the office dress code at the time, and for those three years I shaved my legs dutifully and slid them on. While I had never had to relax my hair to be acceptable in an office, I wore a uniform of sorts. In one boardroom meeting, as graphs and charts detailing market share and competition were set before us by the vice president, I drifted off. First, I surveyed the colour and length of the neckties on the men around the table. Then I tore a tiny hole in my pantyhose with my pen, knowing it would run the length of my leg and I'd need to replace them by the end of the day. A secret rebellion.

I left my job in publishing and have not worn pantyhose since.

Structural power has its symbols. On the chattel slavery plantation, the owners were white. In our current financial structures, owners aren't solely white, but their public presence is coded that way. Black celebrities who undergo surgery to alter their faces; the black musician who claims that slavery was a choice; the black duchess with her straightened hair, who wears 'nude' (for white skin) pantyhose and heels. Power is still white.

My brother's hair is tightly curled and capable of a beautiful afro if he lets it grow, which he did as a teenager. I asked him how he thought such hair functioned in business. He has little time for introspective thoughts on race, he told me; he is caught up in the real race war of economic survival and advancement. He said he'd grown his hair as a teenager to fight the power of the world that didn't like black hair, but nothing has changed. 'I've done all that was asked of me to make it not matter, but it will always matter,' he said. 'I'm always reminded that I vary from the norm and I will never matter.' He's tired of fighting it.

With his words I felt again the need to take us backwards, not forwards — back to that traditional society I once yearned for. Somewhere my grandmother was revered, rather than some place she was running from, where the community was stronger than the pain of failure of the individual. I didn't want the kind of freedom that saw us striving and then hurt, abandoned by the system we were trying to enter. But in that traditional society feet are bound, hierarchies are enforced in different ways. Freedom and tradition still seemed incompatible. So I continue to search for a new path.

I told myself that I was rebelling by poking a hole in my pantyhose, but my step towards freedom, to quitting my job, was tied to my privilege to do so. I grew up in a culture in which freedom is limited to those who can access it. Nevertheless, it fooled me enough to *think* I could become my 'best self'. This cultural belief is the inheritance of a long tradition of European philosophy that fed the rise of modern liberalism in the nineteenth century. In many ancient or traditional societies, the collective good took precedence over individual freedom. Liberty of the individual was identical to collective liberty.

In modern liberal thinking, though, freedom is the ultimate goal. That freedom means glorifying individual achievement and individual desires over collective responsibility. Striding and jumping towards higher heights.

I imagine that the idea of individual freedom served my paternal French ancestor well. Steeped in ideas of liberty from her father's homeland, I imagine her wanting to reinvent herself in Georgetown. Working in her father's shop on Broad Street, her dress indistinguishable from other white ladies in the colony, with her father's Star of David ring now safely disposed of in the trench that runs through the town — only she knows that her family was once in danger. She believes that nothing will ever get in her way again.

But in the twentieth and twenty-first centuries, with neoliberalism spread across the continents, freedom can be bought. This is the freedom of the plantation owner. This freedom requires a hierarchy that pits those who have against those who do not. It requires beating your competitors, beating even the bar itself, jumping over it, time and time again. While war against individual bodies goes on:

A man is arrested on suspicion of selling cigarettes on the street in Staten Island. He holds up his hand and says, 'Don't touch me.' Seconds later he's put in a chokehold. 'I can't breathe', says the man. He dies.

A twenty-nine-year-old migrant worker from Mali in Calabria, Italy, picking oranges by day for a pittance, living in squalor by night in a tent city with other migrants, is gunned down in broad daylight by a white man in a passing car who fires a shotgun at his head.

As they leave a mosque in south London, a pensioner is beaten to death in front of his three-year-old granddaughter by a gang of racist boys too young to be legally named in the media, but not too young to attack him from the front and back, causing him to fall to the ground and suffer a head injury and brain damage. Not too young to kill him.

A teenage woman wearing a hijab is riding the SkyTrain in Vancouver when a white man gets up from his seat, approaches her and threatens to kill her and all Muslims. He strikes her across the face.

An eighty-five-year-old Jewish woman and Holocaust survivor is murdered in her apartment in Paris. After one of the assailants is caught, he says, 'She's a Jew. She must have money', as if that was all the reason he needed.

These accounts remind me of elevator pitches: *boy meets girl, boy gets girl, boy loses girl*. They are sharp and plot-driven, evocative. But my examples are not pitches; they are facts of violence in public against bodies made 'other' and demonised. They are blunt and dramatic, but they also have precursors in the less dramatic racism that people of colour experience every day. These are harder to express in elevator pitches:

The police have a tough job; it's not their fault if they occasionally make a mistake.

All lives matter, not just black lives.

A lot of minorities are too sensitive.

The oranges that the murdered Malian and his migrant co-workers were picking in Calabria are sold to multinational food and drink firms, among them Coca Cola, who manufacture the orange soda called Fanta. Italy's largest farmer association has complained that the prices paid for orange concentrate are unfair, which means they have to hire low-wage migrant workers, who live in run-down buildings, without electricity or water, some without a roof.

No amount of black attainment in such an inequitable system — the so-called freedom of the black musician to make his millions — will erase this violence.

I wonder what makes me strive, what made the high-jumping appealing. I get tired, and yet there is something I have not yet achieved. I believe that my desire for something more is a desire for more connection, not attainment or success.

When I first read Toni Morrison's *The Bluest Eye*, I was still working in publishing. The novel devasted me. Although it is a story in which the most potent symbol is blue eyes and not straight hair or pantyhose, it represents a character's desire for transformation so out of proportion with the possible reality of her life it becomes fantastical, like jumping higher and higher towards heaven.

The Bluest Eye is a shattered, fragmented narrative of shattered, fragmented lives, of violence towards blackness and internalised violence towards the self. The young Pecola, raped by her father, pregnant, and living as a foster child in a family with other young black girls, believes in the contempt with which they are treated.

> You looked at them and wondered why they were so
> ugly; you looked closely and could not find the source.
> Then you realized that it came from conviction, their
> conviction. It was as though some mysterious all-
> knowing master had given each one a cloak of ugliness
> to wear, and they had each accepted it without question.

What keeps Pecola alive ("'Please God," she whispered into the palm of her hand, "Please make me disappear'") is her unrelenting desire for blue eyes like the dolls who are her play companions. Straight hair is attainable: there are combs and chemicals for that. But only God can fulfil her ultimate desire, so each night she prays for blue eyes. Each day she lives in shame and anger, a slow assault on her sanity. In the end, we see Pecola hallucinating herself into survival, believing that her prayers have come true, that her eyes are now blue.

Morrison's depiction of racial self-loathing chimed for me with Ralph Ellison's portrayal of invisibility in the face of desire and aspiration. My life was not one of deprivation like Pecola's. Mine was a childhood in which aspiration and achievement were expected of me. And yet, like Pecola, what I really wanted was not necessarily what I sought. Morrison explores self-loathing and those who 'collapse, silently, anonymously, with no voice to express or acknowledge it. They are invisible.' She and Ellison ask the same question: how are the seeds of racial self-loathing planted?

When I left my publishing job, I moved to Montreal with my partner at the time. In many ways it was a move towards myself. I continued to read as much as I could: post-colonial literature, black literature, James Baldwin, bell hooks. I travelled to Cuba just as it was opening up to tourists. I attended talks and symposia on race and feminism.

At the end of a conference on Caribbean Women at McGill University one hot July day, I waited to see the guest artist give a reading. She was a poet, and I was shy among others in the audience because I knew that I was nothing near a writer yet, despite my desire. The poet was late, and the other conference participants started to leave. I stayed seated in the uncomfortable lecture-room wooden chair, hungry for the words I felt I needed. After more than forty minutes, finally she arrived. I was in awe of her confidence to be late, to be herself no matter who was waiting. The poet was Dionne Brand. She read several poems and I can still feel what they did to the hair on my arms, the feeling they created in my throat, the sense in my feet that I needed to take off my shoes and run towards art. In one poem she listed a contradiction of numbers, the reporting of crimes and accidents against white bodies compared to black bodies. The catastrophe of five or six to the footnote one-liners for the hundreds and thousands. The lists, the numbers, the rhythm, the language, the pain.

Brand gave me permission to talk boldly about bodies in trouble.

At the end of another conference on black women writers a few years later, I crossed paths with a young black woman who looked at me suspiciously, sucked her teeth, and under her breath said, 'Check ye hair, girl.' It dawned on me that she thought my hair had been relaxed, that I was being inauthentic. But I was not relaxed in any way. My hair is flighty and nervous like my heart.

When James Baldwin described why he left the United States for France in 1948, he describes his Paris years as releasing him from how he felt in the US: 'That particular social terror, which was not the paranoia of my own mind, but a real social danger visible in the face of every cop, every boss, everybody.' For me, Baldwin's equation was reversed: I did not experience immediate social danger to my body. My body sent too many mixed messages to the world for that. My danger was really the lack of a place within myself to rest, which created the 'paranoia of my own mind'.

The two boxes with the DNA tests from 23&Me and Ancestry.com have been on my desk for weeks now. I finally open them, follow instructions, spit into one vial and then the other. Then I seal them and mail them off.

My niece, Kiera McWatt. Photo credit: Andrea McFarlane.

5

Ass

dark phrases of womanhood
of never having been a girl
half-notes scattered
without rhythm/no tune
distraught laughter fallin
over a black girl's shoulder

The temperatures in May were the highest since records began in the UK, and June has begun like a fever — the days are long, over sixteen hours; the sun persistent. My terrace plants are constantly thirsty. Everyone is outside in shorts, slinky tops, short dresses that skim the edge of buttocks. Sex is in the air. Sex is in everyone's thoughts. It is already so hot at night that sleeping is difficult — too soon in the summer. In Guyana, June is the beginning of the sugar-cane harvest, before the rainy season. First, the cane fields are burned to remove the leaves, which contain very little sugar. In the tropics, burning crops, burning temperatures: these are a way of life.

I call my mother to ask her whether, as a girl, she saw the sky turn orange with the burning of cane fields; I want to know what she remembers about harvest time. Not much, she tells me, but she proceeds to describe June as a month for dances, as the month she was married in, as a month of romance. She has not lost track of these things the way she has the days of the week.

'What was the name of your boyfriend?' she asks me, and I know which one she means because she has asked several times — the one who came with us on one of our trips to Barbados. A long, long time ago. She doesn't ask me about any of the others.

As we say goodbye she tells me she's happy, which she does frequently, trying to reassure me that she's fine on her own, that she doesn't need me to worry about her, and also making the point that she doesn't want to be moved out of her home. We hang up and I wonder if I should write things down for her, like the names of boyfriends and friends, but then I think that when she asks such questions, she is not looking for facts but for ways to acknowledge me, to connect, because indeed she is happy and fine on her own after so many years of worrying about others.

————

I stopped being a high jumper or competing in track and field when my breasts arrived. Late. Later than most young women. My period didn't come until I was sixteen, and I had been worried it never would. Skinny, flat-chested, without hips or ass, I was boy-like. I was light. I broke records.

The day I got my period I lay on the floor in our dining room, now in a bigger house in a different suburb — a room that was used only on special occasions — because I knew no one would find me there. I held my hands on my pelvis and felt for what was going on inside me, trying to picture it. I was alone. My mother was at work, my sister was away at university, and my grandmother was in her apartment a few miles away — the one I still visited after school every day to feast on her Chinese food and laugh at her imitations. On the day my period arrived, I had yet to tell her about my black runner boyfriend. All those consequences of becoming a woman were in front of me still.

During my girlhood I could ignore the fact that I was female. But now with breasts and a period, I was no longer invisible as a woman. Hormones now presented me with mood swings, and I both longed to return to my twelve-year-old boy body and to be treated like a real woman.

My female role models were my beautiful sister and mother, along with Farrah Fawcett. In my school, there was little escape from images of Farrah. Diana Ross and Cher were alternatives but, at the time, immigrants in the suburbs could not risk being associated with 'wild' girls.

My first sexual experience was also not what I imagine other girls went through. It took place while playing Bach on the cello in the school orchestra. Week after week of rehearsals of the first movement — Allegro — of Brandenburg Concerto No. 3, as I sat in the second cello desk, I was distracted by the double bassist who stood behind me. We shared notes and rhythms, supporting the flurry of the violas and violins with our steady beat and counterpoint, and our bass line held up the melody. He was the best musician in the school and someone I didn't admit to having a terrible crush on because he was beyond reach, a cultured Jewish boy who hung out with the Jewish girls and not with jocks like me. Once, a few weeks into rehearsals, I lost control of my arm and the palm of my left hand slid from the neck of the cello, while the bow in my right hand skipped noisily over several strings.

For fear of the bassist thinking I was rubbish, I became a hopeless cellist. Years later I understood that what had been undermining my playing at every rehearsal was arousal.

Art and sex, I intuited, were about communion, about a connection between people that healed an inherent division between them. Art and sex were places where it was easier to feel a chance of belonging. To me, writing feels like going home, a direct connection to something bigger, outside of myself and yet coming from within me. Romantic relationships challenged my sense of belonging because they involved sharing cultures, and I have never had a single culture to claim. How could anyone other than my siblings relate to *my* background — to the four continents that created me? The plantation house, the cane field, the indenture office, the opium den, the forest, the riverbank, the back room where feet were bound, the tiny cash store: these are not easy spaces of belonging. In Toronto and in London, I find it easier to belong with all the others who do not, like many artists.

To become intimate with someone requires me to trust that I am not serving as a stereotype. In my imagination, my grandmother runs away from rape, but in the colonial imagination, Asian women are racialised and sexualised — evil dragon ladies, erotic lotus blossoms, whores with hearts of gold, China dolls, and submissive mail-order brides. In other stereotypes they are model carers, like the

Filipino migrant workers who raise other people's children, attend to the elderly and the ill, and clean the houses of wealthy people.

The other women in my ancestry — the other symbols of sexuality from the family tree — are as weighted with stereotypes as the China doll. The slave subjected to rape. The indentured servant cosying up to the overseer to reduce her 'coolie bounty'. The 'tragic octoroon' — the stock character of abolitionist literature — who 'passes' as white but whose story ends badly. These women form the images of my womanhood.

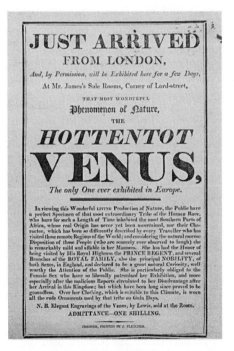

Poster for an 'exhibition' of Saartjie 'Sarah' Baartman, a KhoiSan woman brought to London for 'display'. Source: Wellcome Collection CC BY

In 1810, Saartjie Baartman (originally Sawtche, but renamed by her Dutch owner), a Khoekhoe and San woman from the southern cape of Africa, was brought to London to be exhibited. In the long tradition of human exhibition — which included 'dwarfs' from Sudan displayed in Egypt and 'savages' on display in Europe to justify imperial missions — Khoekhoe women were a great curiosity for colonial collectors of 'natural phenomena' because of the large amounts of fat on their breasts and high up on their buttocks — a 'condition' labelled *steatopygia*, which pathologises it in European terms, although it is not an abnormality in the Khoekhoe people. They wore little or no clothing in their natural environment and have highly developed labia minora.

Her first 'performance' took place at 225 Piccadilly, where the audience was asked to pay two shillings to see this 'Hottentot Venus'. Thrust onto the stage in a skin-tight, transparent outfit adorned by African beads and ostrich feathers, she delighted audiences at a time when England was obsessed with bottoms: Lord Grenville, known for his prodigious backside, and his Whig coalition nicknamed the Broad Bottoms, were poised to take over if King George III had to abdicate the throne due to mental illness.

Sawtche had been sold into freakery, transported, abused, and later sold again to an 'animal exhibitor' who prostituted her, then studied by a French zoologist as the missing link between animals and humans. When she died at only twenty-six, she was subjected to further degradation. Her body was dissected, her brains, genitals and skeleton extracted and studied by the zoologist, who concluded that 'Negroes' were condemned to 'eternal inferiority'. Baartman and her story have many times been used to demonstrate the brutality of scientific racism, but in repeating the focus on her body — continuing to replicate photos and drawings of her — we continue to reduce her to her biology. Negative images perpetuate stereotypes, which perpetuates oppression. When we make a point of seeing some bodies as extraordinary, we make them, again and again, the 'other'.[1]

During the Raj in India, British men found themselves entranced by Nautch girls — dancers who made their living performing pieces derived from sacred Hindu myths. These young women were famous for their delicate features and modesty, and yet one British 'memsahib' wrote in a letter to her mother, 'The native women are as a rule very immoral, but then the religion encourages them in that, for I have read that the Hindoo religion is nothing else but obscenity from first to last.'[2]

And in a more insidious story — insidious because so many children all over the world know it — Peter Pan's Tiger Lily is a native girl of the 'Piccaninny' tribe — a racial slur for a small black child. A loyal friend of the 'boy who won't grow up', Tiger Lily is captured by Captain Hook and left to drown, only to be saved by the eternal boy, with whom she falls in love. She arouses jealousy in Wendy, Peter Pan's true female companion. In depictions of Tiger Lily, she is tied up. In internet spin-offs she is gagged, and even in the Disney movie, there is an undercurrent of the threat of rape.

The images of the women from whom I am descended offered me nothing to fashion my own sexuality on.

How have I been seen? How much racialised baggage have I unknowingly absorbed? I know I have been an object of desire for some black men because of the relative fairness of my skin, which puts me in the master's house rather than out in the sugar-cane field. With equal parts rage and shame I see how plantation dynamics have played out in, and perhaps sabotaged, some of my relationships.

Sex and power. Power and ass. Ass and a dance.

There is a calypso song by Lord Kitchener from my childhood with words to '*wine*' your ass to:

> Audrey, where you get that sugar
> Darling there is nothing sweeter
> You make me scream, you make me bawl
> You make me feel like ten foot tall
> Sugar bum, sugar bum-bum,
> Sugar bum, sugar bum-bum,
> Sugar bum, sugar bum-bum.
> Audrey, every time you wiggle
> Darling, you put me in trouble
> You torture me, the way you wine
> I love to see your fat behind
> Sugar bum, sugar bum-bum.

I love to dance. I dance with abandon around people I know — fully in my body, fully attached to a rhythm that is everyone and everything — and yet in public I hold back. I don't skip along on the street. I don't approach the young women in the park in Kilburn teaching each other moves to ask them to teach me too. I want to laugh and dance in the street like they do, but they don't need me — they are making something powerful for themselves. As a young woman I only rarely danced to calypso, because I didn't have the moves, didn't possess the sway.

I didn't have the ass.

I wanted to be wild, a carnival girl who could shake her booty, but I rejected the objectification. I knew that calypso was often about sex, and as much as I was titillated by the innuendos, I was also embarrassed by them. I felt the hierarchy of the plantation in them.

And now, in the age of black women as superstars, the age of the ass as the re-appropriated site of female power, of the booty fetish and 'shakin' that thang' as ways of taking back sexual control, of upending, so to speak, the objectification and dehumanisation of Saartjie Baartman, I am enthralled by the power over the body that it implies. However, I remain suspicious, and not only because I have little booty to shake. The young women in the park in Kilburn are in control in those moments, but for how long? While I embrace the exuberance of black music, black culture, the effervescence and joy expressed in black bodies when dancing, the energy and space that some black women step into, I can't forget that the booty fetish is rooted in images of domination, in objectification of the body as a means to power, however appropriated. As soon as the moves of those young girls become commodified, something breaks.

During a year I spent living with my artist partner in Paris in the nineties, I became ill. What started as a persistent mild headache became an excruciating pounding behind my eye and burning sensation around it. The skin below my eye began to sizzle with small pustules. My partner had travelled back to Canada for an exhibition and I was alone in a city I felt entirely alien in. I had no health insurance, could not afford to fly back to Toronto, and felt that my French wasn't good enough to go to a French hospital, so I headed to the American Hospital for help.

The doctor who examined me was an attractive blonde woman who seemed genuinely concerned about the rash and blisters appearing on the right side of my face. She asked me where I was born, and I believe she heard Ghana instead of Guyana, because she immediately ordered an HIV test, saying something about African women. I could not quite connect what she said to the rash. I was devastated, horrified.

The blistering continued, my head pounded and soon I looked like I had been punched in the face. In the long rides in the Metro back and forth to the hospital for test after test and to hear the results of those tests, I discovered a strange underground of sexual attention that I had never imagined existed. As I stood on the platform waiting for my train, a French man approached me and asked me if I wanted to go home with him. In the train itself, another man got my attention from across the carriage and motioned that he'd like to kiss me. On the final trip back from the hospital, where tests confirmed that I had shingles rather than AIDS, another man left his seat farther down the carriage to sit next to me and proceed to tell me how he'd look after me.

Was I being propositioned in order to be saved or because I looked like fair game, a woman who was used to being beaten? In this netherworld of sexual exchange, victims had currency, and I was being welcomed as one. Race was colliding with sex and power, silently, stealthily, making me the perfect target.

A few years later, in 1999, I moved to London on my own. It was the London of Cool Britannia, where people from all over Europe, Australasia and Africa were arriving in greater numbers than ever before. The city felt like the Land of Oz for misfits like me who had felt misunderstood, a place where easy kinship among outsiders was found in the streets, in pubs, and on buses. It seemed that everyone was there to participate in something post-colonial and vibrant, a post-dourness, a new era. And as a result of when and where I was born, there was already so much of me here when I arrived. I had, after all, been born British, in a colony on the brink of independence.

The canon of English literature — particularly from the Victorians, a period that coincided with black slavery in the colonies — is packed with images that equate darkness with blackness and that describe African men and women using horror motifs. Joseph Conrad's *Heart of Darkness* was a part of my education in literature, and his storytelling around blackness, savagery, wildness and sex are inescapable: 'The utter savagery ... all that mysterious life of the wilderness that stirs in the forest, in the jungles, in the hearts of wild men.'

Through this dark jungle, a woman moves 'wild and gorgeous'. She carries her head high, her hair is in the shape of a helmet, she is 'savage and superb, wild-eyed and magnificent'. In the hush that falls upon the 'whole sorrowful land, the immense wilderness, the colossal body of the fecund and mysterious life', the woman is one with nature, as though nature is looking at its own 'tenebrous and passionate soul'.

Conrad's narrator admits that the wildness is in all of us:

> The thought of their humanity — like yours — the thought of your remote kinship with this wild and passionate uproar. Ugly... but if you were man enough you would admit to yourself that there was in you just the faintest trace of a response to the terrible frankness of that noise, a dim suspicion of there being a meaning in it which you — you so remote from the night of first ages — could comprehend.

The acknowledgement that 'if you were man enough' you would see the wildness as something inside yourself is the narrator's way of confessing to something he has repressed — a darkness in himself that needs the 'other' to take on that darkness for him.

Images of wildness, sex and being conquered are at the heart of how many women have seen their sexuality portrayed. I have been the 'exotic' object of fascination for some men, and have been confused by their attention. When I first arrived in London, I sought to belong, and felt that a British partner would help me do so. I was in the process of writing my third book, was trying to make enough money to support myself, and to get legal status that would allow me to work in the UK, and I became involved with a man with whom I had little in common but with whom I felt safe. I didn't know then that I was making an exchange – his stability for my 'exotic' presence — but when the relationship fell apart because of our differences, I crashed, there in my small bed in a room in a shared house. I didn't leave it for days. I felt abandoned and like I would never belong anywhere.

I reread Ntozake Shange's *for colored girls who have considered suicide/ when the rainbow is enuf* in those early years in London. It's a book about women who have fallen foul of the myths with which they were raised, and it embraces the poetry of black women's bodies, their truths, their solidarity as black women. The monologues of the women, identified only by their assigned colours (*lady in blue*, *lady in orange*), intersect, making many fragments one whole story of shared pain and joy. In London I wanted my fragments to come together. I wanted to be as alive in all parts of myself as the words on those pages felt, in a sister-hood of feelings. Although I was not suicidal — my work was going well; I had a teaching job; I had an adopted family, children to whom I was another mother, and many friends — I was lonely:

> i am really colored & really sad sometimes and you
> hurt me more than i ever danced outta/into oblivion
> isnt far enuf to get outta this/i am ready to die like a
> lily in the desert/& i cdnt let you in on it cuz i didnt
> know/here is what i have/poems/big thighs

> lil tits/& so much love/will you take it from me this
> one time ...

> ...i dont wanna dance wit ghosts/snuggle lovers i
> made up in my drunkenness/lemme love you just like
> i am/ a colored girl ...

Invited to a literary festival in Jamaica to read from my new novel, I arrived at the resort late in the evening, to bamboo lanterns and soft reggae music. The hosts quickly finished up their dinner to show me to my room on the sea, the waves so close as to nearly lick the cabin. The stars a riot, too much. The air, that air, again on this skin. Too much. I sat in the hammock on my terrace, looked up to the sky and said to myself, Okay, I've been doing this all wrong.

There was no denying where I belonged. I was born of this air, that dark, starlit night. I had been running — or jumping — away from it, trying to belong in places where my body was not at home. I told myself that I needed to find a Caribbean man, someone who would understand that.

The next day, as the other writers arrived, I made progress with my swimming. I had never learned the front crawl, my one failure in high school sports, but I was strong in my breast stroke as I swam in the sea out towards the horizon. I imagined swimming as far as I could, merely to see if I was capable. I had never been able to float except in salt water and had taken to heart the idea that 'black people can't swim'. There in the Caribbean Sea I created for myself a swimming Olympics in salt water.

Later that day, browsing the book stalls, I met an American poet. We began to talk, and the conversation lasted twenty-four hours. He wasn't an instant match for me, but as he unfurled through our conversation the story of his family tragedy, I grew attracted to him. In those twenty-four hours I felt swallowed up by a loving sadness that I believed was a companion to mine.

He was one of three children from a white mother and black father, who had married illegally in the 1960s (the laws against inter-racial marriage were only dropped throughout the United States in

1967). I was drawn to the story, the hybrids and the hardships, and the joy he described in extended family bonds, gatherings, events — similar to that of Caribbean families. Like me, he had a missing brother, but in his case his brother was in jail for life. While my family's loss was unspoken and ghostlike, his was notorious: publicly and privately painful, every single day of his life. We both had survivor's guilt of a sort, neither of us ever feeling like we could fill the place of someone who had been taken from our parents.

I see now that my decision to love him was a decision to save him — from sadness, from loss. I had given myself to writing and he had too. We could share this and our mixed heritages, and we could make new images and narrative lines. If I could save him, make up for our absent brothers, I could save myself.

He lived in the US and I stayed in London. When I visited him in North Carolina I was immersed in African-American culture in a way that my family had never been. The divide between black and white in the US felt so much more acute than in Canada; the 'one drop' rule of blackness meant that there wasn't a question about where I fit there. And yet I was not at home in the southern states — the food, the swagger, the basketball he loved, the hip-hop I loved but that did not reflect my life experience. The fact that I had African ancestry didn't automatically connect me to being an African (north) American.

What I hoped might be a way to bring myself 'home' to my 'real' black identity became yet another struggle for belonging. The poet and I endured transatlantic flights, short visits and long good-byes, hurt feelings in two different time zones, misunderstandings in emails between two writers who could love easily on the page and even in spoken words, but who both kept a little something back from the other, which made real intimacy difficult.

After two years, we both knew it was time for a decision. I took a final trip to North Carolina, reconciled to moving on. We had tried, but neither of us could be expected to change our lives so drastically. Even though he and I were more racially matched than anyone I'd previously partnered with, there were other things that weren't right.

Three weeks after our goodbye, I received an email from him telling me that he needed to speak with me. We arranged for a telephone call that was late in my time zone; by the time we spoke I was very tired. He told me he'd had an epiphany: he would sell his house, move to London to be with me, change his life.

Even as I recognised his declaration of love, I shut down. As we made plans, my doubts grew, but I pushed them aside.

When he arrived, though, I got ill and spent a few days in bed, feeling isolated and alone. I tried hard not to let him know what was going on, but he knew everything about abandonment and loss, and what I did to him, he did to me in return. Perfect abandoners for the lost children inside us.

He shielded himself by writing poetry. I went rollerblading, ate an infinite number of sweets, and returned to the *lady in orange* from Shange's play.

> …/so this is a requiem for myself/…cuz i don't
> know anymore/how to avoid my own face wet wit my
> tears/cuz i had convinced myself colored girls had no
> right to sorrow/& i lived and loved that way & kept

sorrow on the curb/ allegedly for you/but i know i
did it for myself/

i cdnt stand it

i cdnt stand bein sorry & colored at the same time

it's so redundant in the modern world

Lying on the floor alone in my room in the house we were sharing, with him in the room across the hallway, I felt a familiar distress: there were walls, barriers, compartments of my being that no one would be able to penetrate and I would be alone forever. I knew that it was not this man's fault, because I had felt this way in every previous relationship. And this clarity was the only epiphany I needed. My lack of integration could not be pinned on the outside world, on the way it reacted to my hair, my eyes, my skin, my ass.

Two weeks later, I began psychoanalysis.

6

Bones

The arms were a sea of moving antlers. And Gabriel Okimasis, three years old, was perched on a moss-covered rock, the warm breath of a thousand beasts rushing, pummelling, the zigzagging of their horns a cloud of spirit matter, nudging him, licking him with a lover's tongue. And whispering: 'Come with us, Gabriel Okimasis, come with us ...'

When all the bones danced.

The phrase has no context, no story behind it, but it has come to me over the years, haunting me, time and again. The bones rise up out of the earth on their own. They are the bones of all of us. No flesh, no blood. Nothing separating us from each other or the earth.

In the storytelling around race, bones aren't an obvious marker, despite some clichés around size, density and the smiling, water-melon-eating teeth of 'Negro' skeletons. But bones and teeth are potent symbols in the storytelling of ancestry. Fossils are traces of organisms tens of thousands of years old that have petrified. Fossils were animals. Fossils are us. And as such rocks are our ancestors. I am haunted by the potential of their dance.

'The Silence': Clothing and bleached bones were all that remained of this refugee, slain with over 1,000 others at the parish church of Nyarubuye, Rwanda, 1994. Source: Giles Peress/Magnum Photos.

Skeletons are the most naked human form. As a child, before I wanted to be a writer, I had been fascinated by the ancient Egyptians, and had thought of becoming an archaeologist. I wanted to excavate and understand, which is also what writing offers, though at the time I couldn't imagine that my excavation would be with words. For many cultures, human remains are sacred, remnants of ancestors to be revered. Burial grounds fascinated me. Even now, Hamlet's gaze into the empty eye sockets of Yorrick in the gravedigger scene of the play, exploring the Paris catacombs and studying the skeletons of roadkill on the side of an Ontario highway stir in me a thrill at being so close to our physical essence, that dust.

During life, bones shelter vital organs. A broken bone can heal itself.

Deciding to go into psychotherapy was not unlike my fascination with the Chinese Oracle Bone. Looking for help for my repeated bouts of sadness, I sought out a professional who might be able to tell me my future the way the markings on the shoulder blade of a horse would tell a king what to expect from a war. Which particular ancestor of mine was making me so unsettled? I wanted to carve my question into bone and receive an answer I could act upon.

In the weeks and then months that the poet lived with me in London, I was skittish and guilty, ashamed and sorry. Even though I still felt intact as a writer, the rest of me felt unknowable, doomed. I needed to change the story I had been telling about myself to include my failure with intimacy.

I was referred by a friend to a Jungian psychoanalyst not far from where I lived. When I sat in front of her for the first time, I thought, *You'll never get me*. She was a middle-aged, middle-class blonde English woman. Probably fed up with my own roadblocks at that point, I was brave enough to speak up and say, 'I don't think you'll be able to understand me: you're not a black woman.'

She looked at me in a way that was the first of her challenges, then said, with what felt like genuine concern, which I decided to take as provocation, 'Why do you think that?'

I proceeded to tell her about the complexities of my back-ground, the forced intimacy of four continents of which I was the symbolic child, the miscarriage of colonialism. I told her how I had accepted the elements of myself that I considered difficult for anyone to know. The main reason I was there was to discuss the relationship that had just imploded in my tiny room in north London with a mixed-race man from America. How could she, I asked, still very politely, fully understand all of those elements? How could I possibly be helped by her?

She nodded, and took time to consider this. Then quite simply, she said, 'I understand. But maybe you'll explore parts of yourself completely unknown to you yet. And I can be here with you to do that.'

My writerly interest was piqued. I wasn't buying it yet, but we talked for the rest of the session about my history with relationships, and a bit about who my family was. By the end of the session I still wasn't convinced. But things were so tense at my house, I needed someone to talk to, so I returned the following week, and the next and the next. While my therapist kept me centred on who I might be amid the unconscious elements that made up my choices, my relationship slowly and more consciously unravelled. There was an inevitability to its ending, both of us coming to terms with the fact that we'd been in love with each other's poetry, that we had constructed a relation-ship in language rather than a relationship with real intimacy. We had been attracted to the potential to create a story together to repair the loss of our missing brothers, and to create a place of belonging in our mixed racial heritage. But I'd reduced myself and the world to black or white, and that was simply shoddy writing — I couldn't find integrity, let alone happiness.

At first, I resisted the 'selfish' part of therapy — the navel gazing that I interpreted as a right of privilege only. I spoke to her about ideas, about the possibility of justice, equality, fairness and about writing. Rarely did I arrive at her office, the couch looming just to my right like the proverbial elephant in the room, without well-formed narratives of what I'd learned about myself that week. I was determined to solve my issues with love, just like I'd solved everything before, just like I'd jumped higher and higher and set records.

She kept coming back to me being a replacement child, the great hope of a devastated family, and the pressure I would have absorbed. She referred to the trauma my parents faced with the death of their first born, my brother Charles. I had told her the story I'd heard from my mother about how she had retreated into her sorrow, how she and my father became distanced, silently blaming one another and themselves for failing their son, and how she had not allowed my father to touch her for several months until he pleaded with her to make love, saying, 'We must replace this son.' In my father's version of the story he watched my mother suffer, shun him, stay in a darkened room, day upon day, as she was slowly drained of her enchanting spirit. He described their physical reunion by saying, 'And I knew, I just knew' — and he held up his fists as though he had gold pieces in them — 'that we had made you.'

So, I was supposed to fill a hole and heal everything. I was supposed to be a boy. I proceeded to try to fulfil this destiny. Impossible. Sad.

It was a revelation to realise that the missing thing inside me might be the missing thing inside my parents. The question my teacher asked me in grade three singled me out as the word no one else in the room was or even knew. But we all have some sort of hole inside us that we're seeking to fill. My therapist relieved me of the burden of thinking that the hole was my fault, which also gave me responsibility for myself and how I choose to interpret my experiences.

It was not simple to untangle my reactions and my private, mostly unconscious, storytelling around self-worth from my family's story-telling or society's. The same false narratives used to justify enslavement — telling us that biology is destiny and that white is primordial — also inhabit European psychoanalysis and certainly Jungian concepts. Jungian analysts interpret the 'shadow' (the unconscious, those aspects of the self that are unacknowledged or unknown consciously) using the language of darkness, blackness and otherness. Still, writers like Frantz Fanon have used psycho-analysis and psychoanalytic theory to explain the degradation and inadequacy experienced by colonial subjects. The black man's expe-rience of racism is not unconscious — it is out in the open. These feelings 'make his drama' says Fanon. A white man, on the other hand, has been able to make his racism unconscious because 'a new element appears: guilt'. Or indeed shame. Fanon was able to turn psychoanalysis back on its creators, to reveal the 'sickness' of the division between white and black.

The first time my therapist analysed a black person who figured in one of my dreams as the 'shadow', I challenged her. I told her it was a racist idea, perpetuated through centuries of so-called science in the service of slavery. I felt personally affronted and thought of quitting her. How could we escape the racist ideology of the era in which Jung and Freud developed their theories? But I didn't quit, because I felt that we were both struggling towards something beyond language. She came back to the topic the following week, acknowledging to me that the language of the archetypes did bear historical racism. But archetypes, she said, were meant to help identify parts of the self that the patient hadn't yet faced. And so I focussed on language and began to use the racist language of psychoanalysis against itself. I became interested in this image: the slave was part of the slave master; black only existed because of the white state of mind, and black was the embodiment of the greatest fears of that state of mind.

She never again used blackness in that way, and I believe we taught each other something. Much later in the analysis, when the formality between us had been erased, I found out that her favourite book was *Jane Eyre*. By this point, I felt that my Bertha Mason had influenced her Jane, and that we had co-created a story that somehow brought us closer together in the therapeutic sense. That meant I had access to both Jane and Bertha, that I was less divided. Intimacy was attainable.

I felt inwardly free. My writing flowed more easily. I shed the need for attainment. I realised I did not need to identify with one ethnicity or another, with one tradition or another. Freedom was not in opposition to tradition after all; the two had nothing to do with one another. As a result of the insights I gained in therapy, my politics became more about ensuring that those whose stories were suppressed were heard than the politics of group identities.

Audre Lorde, American poet, also speaks of light and dark when she talks about women's voices. She tells us:

The quality of light by which we scrutinize our lives
has direct bearing upon the product which we live,
and upon the changes which we hope to bring about
through those lives …

As we learn to bear the intimacy of scrutiny and
to flourish within it, as we learn to use the products of
that scrutiny for power within our living, those fears
which rule our lives and form our silences begin to
lose their control over us.

For each of us as women, there is a dark place
within where hidden and growing our true spirit rises
…

These places of possibility are dark because they
are ancient and hidden; they have survived and grown
strong through that darkness.

Darkness gives us a way forward.

Lorde was among those who helped create the identity politics
of the late 1970s, a necessary movement for black women who
challenged the image of feminists as white and 'workers' as white
males. The Combahee River Collective, which she helped to found,
was an organisation of black feminists who brought black women's
concerns into focus. In their view, oppression of various groups was
interlocking; they were among the first to articulate the intersec-
tions of oppression among gender, class and race. The movement
grew to include others for whom the feminist movement was not
speaking, disability groups and transgender groups among them.

Over the last few decades, the people who make up the complex web of identities outside of the main circles of power have become more vocal and visible.

By focussing on my racial and gender identity, I was able to grow into myself — to see myself as others saw me and to embrace that vision. But as I watch new 'identities' form against social power structures, I see that the power itself doesn't shift. Some white men now claim to be oppressed for being white men. Structural inequality seems unchanged, and the new 'plantation owners' — the minority of people around the world with the largest percentage of the global wealth — enjoy unfettered power by keeping us divided. Identifying as a woman of colour has been crucial in my understanding of structural politics in society. But this focus hasn't changed the plantation structure, the violence against black bodies and women's bodies. A racial identity can be used against us, to keep us in our category, to keep us divided. When we are so divided, it appears that it is impossible to address inequality, because it looks as though we're calling for 'sameness' and not equality. Which is, of course, not what we want at all.

Therapy allowed me to shed light on how I could be responsible for myself and put myself forward into the world to be a part of change; it showed me that my identity was deeper than race, gender, sexuality, class or ability. It gave me the freedom to begin to tell stories about my existence that weren't attached to race. It helped me to identify old ones — the metaphorical high jumper and the unhappy saviour of sad men — so that I could discard them.

When my American partner finally moved out of the house, I was relieved. I vowed I would learn to swim well. I joined a gym and went daily. Since I could not afford lessons because I was paying for therapy, I watched others swimming and taught myself. By the following year I was breaking my own records again, in the pool this time, doing the front crawl, breathing on both sides, gliding through the water with newfound buoyancy.

Myths around race and sports are attached to the way we talk about the so-called difference in structure of black and white bodies — black people can't swim or play tennis; white people can't dance or play basketball.

Before Venus and Serena Williams, tennis was not considered something that black people could excel at. Few people talk about Althea Gibson, the first black athlete to 'cross the colour line' in international tennis, winning the Grand Slam title at the French Open in 1956. The stories we choose to keep alive say a lot about the culture we create. Before Simone Manuel, the gold medal winner and record holder in the 100-metre freestyle at Rio in 2016, Olympic swimming was not considered an area of elite-level competition for people of colour. Even after Venus and Serena took over the tennis world and Serena challenged the record for the numbers of grand slam wins in the game, she still was subjected to racist attacks. Sports commentators racialised her body, often referring to her buttocks. 'On some women [the catsuit] might look good. Unfortunately, some women aren't wearing it. On Serena, it only serves to accentuate a superstructure that is already bordering on the digitally enhanced and a rear end that I will attempt to sum up as discreetly as possible by simply referring to it as "formidable",' said Otis Gibson of the

Australian *Sunday Telegraph*. In a Tweet, one spectator went even further: 'Looks like a gorilla, and sounds like a gorilla when she grunts while hitting the ball. In conclusion, she is a gorilla.' The surfacing of the despicable, dehumanising legacy of slavery.

The myth that black people can't swim as well as white people due to heavier bone density — a myth to which I had subscribed as I flailed in the swimming pool in high school — does not explain the absence of black people from pools or lakes in North America. There is little need to look further for the origins of that idea that black people can't swim than the slaves tossed over the sides of ships in the Atlantic. Black bodies, dead or alive, thrown overboard in the middle passage, *wasted cargo*, flailing, drowning, sinking slowly into the dark, to make 'bone soldered to coral by bone'.[1] Slavery and the sea, bones and dark water. Heavier because of the sheer number of bodies. Even as they murdered them, the slave traders would ask their insurance companies for compensation for the loss of those same bodies.

Yet there is more: all those decades of exclusion from public pools in North America, because of Jim Crow laws, as they were called. During segregation in the United States, blacks and whites were legally forbidden from marrying, from sharing railroads, libraries, buses and schools, and from fishing, boating and bathing together. In Alabama in 1930, a law was introduced that stated, 'it shall be unlawful for a Negro and white person to play together or in company with each other in any game of cards or dice, dominoes or checkers'.

These laws varied from state to state, but all of them were designed to exclude, denigrate and punish African-Americans. Even now, long after the laws were abolished, the spirit of segregation lingers. In the wake of desegregation, white communities became fearful of shared black and white spaces, believing that public pools were sites of communicable 'black' diseases, and suspicious of black men and white women nearly naked in close contact. Instead of opening up the pools to blacks, many communities in Alabama closed down public pools altogether, filling them in, cementing over them.

Wasted cargo.

After my breakup, after beginning therapy, after learning to swim, I felt different. Always, when I had returned to Canada on my twice annual visits for holiday, literary events or work, my divisions threatened to rear up, because home was a place where I had been an immigrant trying to fit in. But with a different sense of myself, and an additional sense of being a European, my perceptions of the country changed. I saw it as an outsider might — the space, the big skies, the feeling of freedom from the weight of European history and its ancient class divisions, and the promise in its youthfulness.

Without the pressure of assimilation, I also saw more clearly how shameful the country's relationship with its indigenous people was.

As a child, I'd been steeped in the stereotypes of popular films, casual reference to the 'Indian problem' and the skewed history of the settlement of Canada that left out the real consequences of colonialism on the indigenous people. Every year of my childhood, Canada Day celebrations praised the country's origin story, leaving out the still unresolved issues around land claims and the atrocities of the residential school system. As a result, children like me could look away from the disenfranchised people on the streets of downtown Toronto and drive through First Nations reserves without fully appreciating that here were people whose land and culture had been stolen. In the country's centennial in 1967, I wore my 'pioneer girl' costume at school, blind to the fact of the cultural genocide of Canada's indigenous people. When I look at this photo now, I laugh, but I am also confounded by the collective blindness I was once part of.

One hundred years of Canadian Confederation, celebrated in my elementary school, with my sister the saloon girl, my brother the cowboy, and me the hardworking pioneer woman.
Source: Family photo.

As a child I had been taken for a 'Native' several times while camping in Ontario with my family, and when I was thirteen at service station stops on the long drive across the country to visit the Calgary Stampede, Lake Louise and Banff National Park.

We stopped in Lethbridge, Alberta, to watch a local baseball game. When I sat near some local boys in the bleachers, they goaded one another until one boy came to sit next to me. While he pretended to be watching the game with his arms crossed, he slyly poked me, just missing my breast, his real target. Before I could do anything but flinch in shock, he bolted, scrambling down the steps of the bleachers with the other boys. As they teased each other, I heard the words 'dirty squaw'— no doubt intended for my ears. *Dirty squaw, black bitch. Then and now.*

In the back seat of our 1970 Pontiac Catalina with my sister, watching out the window as we drove through First Nations reserves, I did notice that my family looked more like we belonged here than in the suburbs of Toronto. But I didn't realise that our car had been named for an indigenous warrior who had led a resistance against British occupation and for whom a war in 1763 against the British was named. On that cross-country road trip, ironically, we felt we were becoming 'true Canadians', and at the Calgary Stampede we all proudly wore cowboy hats.

Recently, at my sister's cottage during a summer holiday in Ontario, I swam into an ancient image. I was doing my usual lengths between the dock and a small island about a pool's length away. As I neared the island I felt something around my ankle, which I thought was a weed. I tried to shake it off, only to feel it return. I shook again, and then as I swam harder to pull away, something bit hard into my ankle and held on. I panicked, sure that I was being bitten by a large snake or a giant snapping turtle, or a giant eel with a mouth so large it could take my entire ankle into its jaws. Snake! Snake! I screamed, and then, feeling like the thing was pulling me down into the dark lake, 'I'm drowning, I'm drowning!' My brother heard and came for me in a rowboat. When he pulled me up into the boat, I was certain that he would bring the creature with me — some sort of prehistoric lake beast that no one had ever known existed.

It turned out that the thing attached to my ankle was a fishing lure nearly a foot long, its three sets of large hooks embedded deeply into my flesh. It was fish-shaped, designed to catch a Muskie, a rare species prized by fishermen. To be so wounded in the water was a blow for someone who had believed that learning to swim had freed me. But also, rising up in me, was the more ancient image of black bodies in water, wasted cargo. In Jungian analysis, water is also the dreamscape of the dangerous, dark depths of the unconscious — to top it off, the lake I'd been swimming in is called *Shadow* Lake.

Paramedics took me to the hospital in an ambulance, where a doctor removed the lure. But he didn't prescribe antibiotics. Two days later, an infection took hold that turned my foot and ankle a glowing red. I went to the local pharmacist to ask for advice. I was dishevelled, limping, my skin darkened from days on the dock at the lake; the pharmacist scrutinised me as I approached, but as I reached her she looked away, busying herself with something behind the counter. 'Excuse me,' I said, and she still didn't look up. Finally, I spoke a little louder, asking her if she could help me by checking out my foot to see if it was infected. At last she met my eyes, but she was clearly irritated. I started to explain again but lost my composure, reverting to the small child who wanted to become invisible. My sister came to my rescue. When she told the woman she was a local resident, also managing to mention her professional status, the pharmacist loosened up, looked at my foot and told me, yes, it was infected.

After we left, my sister and I talked about what had just happened. I told her about a trip I'd taken with three friends — two men, one woman, all white — in the summer of my first year in university. When we'd paired up and were hitchhiking from Edmonton to Northern Saskatchewan to spend a week in a remote cabin, the other couple had no trouble getting rides, while my hitchhiking partner and I stood for hours with our thumbs out. As the sun went down, we had to walk to a motel and get a room for the night. The next morning we took a bus.

As my sister and I drove to the hospital, we spoke of how being brown in rural North America is a hazard. Once again we mentioned our awe that our father had left his unhappy life working in animal inspection for the Canadian government in Toronto to retire to a farm. He bred horses, raised cattle and, later, at a different farm grew asparagus and strawberries. Scrutinised and rejected by the local Rotary Club, he persisted, sold his crops, made a living for over twenty years. We remembered how we'd never seen people of colour when we camped as children, or other black people who owned farms or worked on the land, though, as adults, in cottage country we had seen Vietnamese people picking worms by night to make a living. Of course, we both knew that people had run from the land to the city to escape slavery, and we understood our father's defiance in doing this in reverse, but we also imagined the daily humiliation he would have absorbed as though it were normal. And still, this was nothing compared to the experience of indigenous people on their own land.

On my return summer visits, I saw how plantation dynamics function outside of the plantation itself, and how hierarchies, land rights, labour and shame make up the current inequalities. When I tell people that a part of my heritage is 'Amerindian' they sometimes ask how much, as though it indicates a percentage of oppression or belonging. I am an immigrant to Canada, and yet my life there has been 'white' in comparison to First Nations people.

I recognise that I have always been drawn to the spirituality and reverence for nature that I identified in First Nations stories I learned growing up in Canada, but given the striking erasure of the genocide that took place at first contact with Europeans from my education, I also recognise that this simplistic sense of 'native spirituality' and the 'reverence for nature' is part of a racist and reductive interpretation of indigenous communities.

But still, so much is wrong with how we — most industrial nations around the world — structure our relationship to nature. We treat nature and its riches as something to own, to harvest, to make *other* and not us. And in this we foster the plantation.

My identity has been carved out of an otherness that is indivisible from every single othering that has gone on in history — the act of othering, repeated time and again. I see how race serves the plantation, the empire, the board room, the pulpit, or wherever race-making is taking place. The plantation likes identity politics. It likes us to be divided while it continues to make profits.

So I resort again to my imagination.

My indigenous ancestor? She's a woman who rises with the

sun, stands on the bank of a river with a bow and arrow and shoots fish for her family's dinner. She doesn't own the land or live on it; she lives with it. She is fast, lithe, does not like to be pinned down. She has a lot in common with warrior women all around the world, and she doesn't choose to divide herself from them based on this particular river or this particular fight for survival as the bulldozers pull into the forest behind her.

Indigenous literature in Canada is steeped in acts of defiance. Tomson Highway's plays of the late 1980s, *The Rez Sisters* and *Dry Lips Oughta Move to Kapuskasing,* were daring, shocking pieces of theatre that represented things I hadn't heard many Canadians talk about before. The plays were about life on First Nation reserves and they mirrored what we saw when we drove through northern Ontario and the prairie provinces on our travels — neglect, dereliction, the ravages of alcohol — but they also opened up vistas of meaning, of desire, hope and dreaming, and of a different way of looking at the body and its spirit.

Highway's novel, *The Kiss of The Fur Queen*, has dreaming at its core. In his introduction, Highway tells us about the dream-world of his people, by introducing us to the Trickster, a figure as important as Christ for Christians. Weesageechak in Cree, Nanabush in Ojibway, the trickster has many guises, straddles the consciousness of humans and the Great Spirit, and teaches us about the nature and meaning of existence on the earth. This figure is similar to Anansi, the trickster character in Caribbean literature who has a similar function and also can take on different forms, genders, animal natures.

Highway asks if Cree and other First Nations languages have no gender, then why should we? 'And why, for that matter, should God?' The trickster is gender fluid, and fluidity follows in all aspects of life. For Highway, 'trees are *who* not *what*'. The trickster is everywhere and in everything. And there are no borders between people and nature.

In the novel, Gabriel Okimasis and his brother Jeremiah — their first names changed from Oooneemeetoo and Champion by the Christian residential school where their own language is forbidden — are sexually abused by priests. Out of this trauma are born two artists: a dancer and a musician. The novel uses the brothers' bodies as a landscape of colonial abuse — the dancer felled by it; the musician isolated. Highway's fiction is alive not only with the tragedy of the lost Cree culture it describes, but with the force of resistance, through dance and music, through the pow-wow dance that seems to come from beyond, from ancestors, from something eternal.

> Like a thunderclap, silence struck. Jeremiah leapt
> from his bench, and with a beaded drumstick
> pounded at the bass strings of the instrument. The
> quintet of circling dancers launched into a pentatonic
> chant, '*Ateek, ateek, astum, astu, yoah, ho-ho!*' And,
> suddenly, the piano was a pow-wow drum propelling a
> Cree Round Dance with the clangour and dissonance
> of the twentieth century.
>
> ... Through the brothers, as one, and through
> a chamber as vast as the north, an old man's voice
> passed. 'My son,' it sighed, 'with these magic
> weapons, make a new world ...'

The novel resists the colonial legacy of residential schools through collective memory, through art and dance. When Gabriel dances, he executes 'a turn so nimble witnesses swore later that he had outwitted gravity, then snapped into a robot-like march to a circle of blue-white light ...'

This is what I long to do: to speak beyond an identity that was named for me. I want to write towards light and the moment when all the bones dance.

7

Skin

The story of the little boat that crossed the
river night after night, and who was in it.
The story of a man and woman, standing
together in the moonlight. Skin to skin.

Skin is our largest organ, the unique size of our individual bodies.
It is the organ of touch. When we blush or are hot or cold, it gives
us away. It shows when we are excited or repulsed. Like the rings in
tree trunks, it reveals the life we've lived — our scars, our wrinkles
forming where we are most susceptible to irritation or unhappiness
or surprise or laughter. Skin is our life's record.

It can be grafted to heal wounds; it can be donated to other bodies. In this sense, it can live apart from us, beyond our natural lives. It
can be a canvas for art. There is no other organ that changes colour
regularly, that does so much to protect us, and yet is abused or under-
appreciated to such an extent. No other organ is the frontier between
the outside world and our insides. No other organ is used against us.

Early anatomists saw skin as having little value, and flayed it to reveal the more important workings of the body beneath it. But in the seventeenth century, anatomists like Jean Riolan the Younger became curious about the source of blackness within African skin. Riolan blistered the skin of a black African body with a chemical agent, then removed the seared specimen to examine its layers. A similar experiment later that century identified the actual layer of skin where dark pigmentation is found; another anatomist even asserted that blackness came from 'dark scales'.

Early anatomists disregarded skin as an important organ.
Source: Juan Valverde de Amusco, 1559 — Copperplate engraving.
National Library of Medicine, Rome.

Today we know that skin needs melanin to protect it from being destroyed by UV rays from the sun, and these natural pigment levels vary. Dark skin is dark because it has a higher percentage of eumelanin than lighter skin. Dark skin is the product of a survival mechanism that helped early human species who moved out of the rainforest and onto sunny savannahs to survive. Darkness is a means of evolution; it is necessary in relation to light.

But a congenital disorder can result in the reduction or absence of melanin pigment, and a black person can appear white-skinned. For me, this porous quality is the most potent image of skin as the barrier between so-called races. Skin as a marker of race is a false border — merely an illusion of a border between us and the outside world, between us and other bodies.

Psychoanalysis gave me language around dark and light in which racial blackness was only possible because of the white state of mind that feared it most. It offered an explanation for racism and allowed me to look beyond it. Jung's language of dream interpretation became another world-building tool for me to use in storytelling, a way of understanding life through language and a way to dissect human interaction. I was in it for the process of excavation.

All systems of belief — Eastern and Western, the dharmic and the evangelical — involve storytelling, with myths and legends, heroes, warriors, lovers, victims and conquerors. Most systems get stuck in a single story, but in psychoanalysis the most important thing is the process itself, the sharing, the self-reflection, the healthy distance that can be found when one tells one's own tale, over and over again, with the *findings* themselves being less significant. Similar to writing, the story of the self is true in each particular telling. We change, the story unfolds and changes, but the telling itself is eternal.

My sense of being whole after analysis increased my feeling of being porous to people around me. Instead of putting up barriers to intimacy, feeling like I didn't belong anywhere and that I had to protect my corner, I felt more belonging. I felt even more love and more suffering. I felt more from and for other people — my family, friends, colleagues, strangers in the same tube carriage, crowds in photos, individuals in the news, students in my office, grizzled men sitting on the pavement. Feeling responsible for myself, I was able to be more generous to others. My focus shifted from inward to outward. My happiness was still not possible while black and brown and yellow and red bodies and women's bodies and less-able bodies and queer bodies and poor bodies were still targets of neglect, hatred, violence. I knew I had to demand responsibility in others.

Police pull a black man over because his car is missing a taillight. The man gets out of the car and runs. Police shoot him in the back.

A white man on neighbourhood watch shoots a young black man for looking 'suspicious'.

A white woman brandishes a ten-inch knife, screaming 'I want to kill all you Jews' as she chases Jewish children outside a synagogue.

A government puts brown children in cages.

A brown woman who is thirty-four weeks pregnant is on a bus with her children where she is abused by white passengers for not speaking English. 'Sand rats, ISIS bitches,' they say. 'Go back to your fucking country where they're bombing every day ... You're lucky I don't kick you in the uterus and you'll never have a baby again.'

A black man is physically restrained on the plane flight that is deporting him. His arms are handcuffed behind his back, seatbelt tight, he is bent over in an impossible position. 'Please let me go... you're killing me, please help.' Thirty-five minutes later he is dead.

A young indigenous woman is followed in the street by police who suspect she is a sex-worker. Arrested for public intoxication, she is subjected to hours of violent humiliation, sexual abuse, an officer's knee in her kidney. Her hair is grabbed, her shirt and bra cut off, and she is left naked in her cell.

I can't breathe.

I am a social being committed to others. I first found a sense of political identity through women's groups and the politics of women of colour. I later identified with other marginalised groups fighting for recognition, inclusion and rights, connecting their struggles with my own family's history and experience. Our current struggles have precedents: in slave rebellions, among the suffragettes, in the civil rights movement and the hard-won battles of representation and rights for racial, gender, religious, ability groups in a slow awakening, over decades, of 'otherness' against the centre. That diverse world we imagined in the 1970s, with everyone singing in unison, has not come into being. The centre still holds.

Released from the fog of sadness that characterised my youth, I now also felt unprecedented anger. I re-invigorated my allegiance with political blackness. And it had broadened. Connection to the self that therapy brought didn't mean selfishness — it isn't about self-actualisation at all costs. It isn't about a particular way of look-ing at freedom. I look back to that plantation I imagined, where my ancestors undertook various forms of coerced labour and I think about why its structure still governs, why that structure is so deeply a part of our economic reality. James Baldwin famously said, 'What white people have to do is try and find out in their own hearts why it was necessary to have a nigger in the first place, because I am not a nigger, I am a man. But if you think I'm a nigger, it means you need him.' Why do we still need a 'nigger'?

I oppose the treatment of people as chattel, oppose neglect, oppose the lowest price for the lowest labour, oppose coercion and manipulation, oppose exploitation, oppose cages and shackles and shanty towns and ghettos and the borders of race-making. If white is a state of mind that allows the plantation to flourish, with black as its opposite, my politics define my 'colour'. If I put white on the psychoanalyst's couch, I see that, yes, it urgently has to deal with its shadow, with the reason for the existence of blackness, with the divisions between us that are creating so much pain. I remember what my therapist said that first day when I challenged her on not being able to understand me: 'But maybe you'll explore parts of yourself completely unknown to you yet.'

That's an exciting prospect for all of us to face together.

It's hot in London and has been hot for over two months, with only occasional bouts of rain in the night, which remind me of Canadian summer rain — hard downpours, buckets of rain. In this normally grey, drizzly country, buckets of rain feel out of place, damaging the roses, drowning low-lying towns, creating a new leak in my roof.

In early July it is usually still green in the parks and gardens, but not this year. I am looking forward to my month in Canada, the lake swims, the cool woods of Ontario, and even the air conditioning in the city, where the summer also has been exceedingly hot.

I walk through my neighbourhood park on a Saturday. England has had a breakthrough in the football World Cup, and the city is electric with hope. Children's parties fill the corners of the park, with toddlers running about, ignoring the calls of parents too hot to chase after them. Families, black and brown and white and mixed, lay out food for their picnics. Even on a day like today, thirty degrees celsius, there are people lying in the sun. All of these sunbathers are white. The English are known for their sun worshipping, and little wonder, but today it feels misguided.

I am tired, my mind muddled, because sleeping is hard in the heat. My apartment is airless in the middle of the night, even with every window open as wide as it will go. I live at the top of a house and sounds come from all directions below me — the cries and raised voices, the motorbikes and the radios. In the night I hear voices in languages I do not recognise and a few that I do. Men arguing. One night I heard a slap that seemed to come right into my window. Then there were more voices, raised in excitement, or maybe in alarm. There were repeated slaps, a ritual of slapping, flesh against flesh. Perhaps a beating, perhaps a loving. I put a pillow over my head.

As I walk through the park and look at the skin of the white people in the sun, I think I can see it cooking. The grass is brown, leaves are wilted and the sky is yellow, not summer blue. In Canada's capital, Ottawa, the temperature and humidex have hit forty-seven degrees celsius. Seventy deaths in Montreal have been attributed to the heat. In the Caucasus mountains it has been over forty degrees and the region has experienced major power cuts as people crank up the air conditioning to keep cool. In Japan, the heatwave has been declared a natural disaster because of the mounting death toll. Greek woods are burning; Southern California wildfires are raging.

I touch my neck. My fingers wipe away the perspiration there, and I press down on my collarbone, rubbing my own sweat in like a lotion. I love heat and am happiest in the summer, but this heat wave has frightened me; icebergs are melting, the big Arctic thaw is coming. I wonder why we are allowing these effects to continue. I sit under a tree and wipe my neck again. I scratch the sweaty skin under my watch and notice the tan line formed only in the last few days.

Because I live mostly in the north, particularly in England, renowned for its lack of sunlight, my skin can appear very fair. Once I get enough melanin as protection, though, my skin can get darker and darker, and then I am mistaken for a Mexican or a Brazilian or an indigenous American. A friend in London once referred to me as a 'light skinned' black girl and, like the moment when my Canadian friend identified me as 'socially white', I felt removed from my blackness. My black skin was lightened through miscegenation, but in even acknowledging different shades of blackness, we engage in what C. L. R. James in *The Black Jacobins* calls the 'tom foolery' of identifying quadroons or octoroons or any traces of African heritage. Because the truth is that the dominating fact of a plantation society is 'fear of the slaves'.

My sister became the first woman of colour to be superior court judge in Ontario. I am enormously proud of her achievements, her intelligence and her tireless, dedicated work, but I wonder if she would have been able to shatter those barriers if her skin had been darker. As a young girl she had been pushed down in the playground and called 'nigger', but her skin is fair, her nose petite, her hair tamed and 'respectable'. Studies suggest that skin tone and socioeconomic achievement are twinned. Lighter-skinned members of racial minorities enjoy higher average levels of education, income, and occupational status than darker skinned members. And light is associated with intelligence, trustworthiness, beauty.[1]

In my twenties in Toronto I was perpetually included in racist conversations in which people, mostly colleagues or strangers, talked about black people as though I wasn't one. If they acknowledged my otherness or blackness at all, they treated me as if I was exempt or was aligned with them against something else that they were naming. They 'didn't mean me', which is a classic (*'Oh, no,' my teacher said, 'Not Tessa. Tessa's something else'*) racist response. Normally, though, I thought my friends understood who I was. Then a friend whose background was eastern European one day told me that she wanted to move out of the neighbourhood she was living in because there were 'too many black people'. I can't remember how I responded or if I did at all. I only know that after many years of friendship I could no longer tolerate her company, not only because of the racist remark, or the sense that my shade of blackness had protected me throughout our friendship, but because I realised that she had not seen who I was at all — a case of mistaken identity. Or, worse, I had mistaken my own identity.

Skin lightening has long been practised in many parts of the world. The widespread use of chemical skin lighteners — containing mercury, corticosteroids and hydroquinone, which is used to suppress melanin production — is a desperate reach to be free of the negative perceptions of blackness. Globally, too, skin colour and social status are linked, with paler skin associated with wealth and spending a life sheltered indoors, and darker skin associated with those who toil under the sun. And, as one user of lightening products said, 'You grow up knowing that the lighter ladies are the prettier ones. It's just a fact.'[2]

In Mali, Nigeria, South Africa, Senegal, Indonesia, India, Canada, the US, the UK, Brazil, Korea, Japan and China among other places, products such as Black and White Cream, Nadolina,

Ambi, Palmer's, Swiss Whitening Pills, Ultra Glow, Skin Success and Clear Essence, and a Cameroon pop singer's favourite, Whitenicious, are sold to people — mostly women — who long for not necessarily white skin, but the 'light' skin of African-American celebrities like Beyoncé or Bollywood actresses like Isha Koppikar or Aishwarya Rai. In the multi-billion dollar industry of skin lightening, many products are sold to people who claim to want to even out their skin tone, to 'get rid of spots'. Many seek healthier alternatives to the chemical lighteners, those that claim to be based on ayurvedic medicine and ingredients such as saffron, papaya, almonds and lentils. More Western versions claim to contain Vitamin C and Glutathione, and all produce varying results: *I'm so disappointed … not even one shade lighter.*

Long term use of hydroquinone can lead to ochronosis, a disfiguring condition that leaves the skin puckered with yellow banana shaped fibres, caviar-like papules and dark pigmentation. Overuse of topical steroids can lead to contact eczema, bacterial and fungal infection, an adrenal gland disease called Cushing's syndrome, along with skin thinning and kidney disease.

The Caribbean man at Speaker's Corner in Hyde Park in 1956 was prescient when he pointed his finger at the white people in the crowd and proclaimed 'We gwon brown y'all up'. Not in the way he might have meant at the time, but with skin lighteners browning up darker hues.

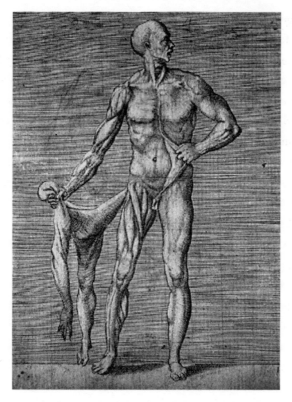

Anatomist's drawing. What lies beneath. Source: The Elisha Whittelsey Collection, The Elisha Whittelsey Fund, 1949.

While my psychoanalysis deepened, wavered, weakened, became more and less important over years and normalised into my life like regular exercise, I zeroed in on material inequality as the main narrator of race-making. I am relatively free to choose my course in life because I had believed in a liberal dream of being self-made. Yet by following that dream I bought into the plantation hierarchy that established that freedom would come if I strove to work in the master's house. In Canada and the UK there have been many multiculturalism and diversity initiatives, but the structures haven't changed. As Audre Lord said, the master's tools will never dismantle the master's house.

Diversity programmes, affirmative action and attention to representation in work, government and culture are crucial in reaching towards equality, and yet these initiatives are contentious and are often accused of lowering standards or creating reverse discrimination. The opposition to them doesn't take into account the history of inequality, nor does it include an understanding of how privilege functions.

As it is in the Caribbean, race is a complex matter in Brazil, where people have many names (*Brancos, Pardos, Pretos, Caboclos, Amarelos, Indigenous*) for the shades and identities of Brazilians. There, as elsewhere, class plays a big part: 'Money whitens' is a common phrase in the country.

In the Caribbean after slavery, the black, yellow, brown and red mix of faces and skin existed in a hierarchy climbing towards white, towards the plantation house and not the sugar-cane field. A similar effort to 'whiten' its population, had been in play in Brazil since abolition. Doctors and lawyers were primarily lighter skinned, while bus drivers and domestic servants were black.

While the country had always prided itself on a thousand shades of brown, in 2014 Brazil acknowledged the legacy of slavery in its institutions and the white supremacy it was founded on, and passed affirmative action laws to increase non-white enrolment in public universities and non-white managers in the civil service. The aim was to increase the black elite in Brazil to twenty per cent by 2024.

The government established a quota system. Many people who had previously identified as white — under fifty per cent of the population — had some African or indigenous ancestry and signed up to the quota system in order to gain access to education or jobs. And the administration soon ran into problems with 'racial fraud'. People with white features checked the 'black' box on applications and got quota places at universities, which angered others who looked 'more black' and were refused places. As a solution to the abuse of the system, the government introduced an anti-fraud commission, in which a panel of judges determines if the applicants are in fact black or indigenous. This is not an easy task in such a racially mixed culture as Brazil. As my own mixed background demonstrates, both identification from the outside and identity from the inside are deeply subjective, based on any one person's understanding of looks, skin or heritage. Asked by an interviewer what he thought were the features of his blackness that would make him eligible for a government job, one candidate said that he searched for his skin tone on Wikipedia and decided he was dark enough. Another suggested that even though he had 'white' hair, his lips and nose made him black. Another candidate asked, 'My nose is not that big. Does that mean I'm not black?'

In a reversal of 'passing' as white to gain social advantage, Brazil now has more people ticking 'black' on questionnaires in order to get jobs. Before the new racial consciousness brought by the affirmative action programmes, light-skinned black people who would be considered black in the US were generally not considered black in Brazilian society. In Brazil, race has not been about roots. If you look black you are black; if you look white you are white. Two siblings could call themselves two different things, depending on how they look. They could have black, white and mixed cousins.

While the affirmative action programmes in Brazil don't, in Lorde's phrase, 'dismantle the master's house', they offer a different way of seeing. A broadcaster asked a government official on the anti-fraud panel how they would know 'who is black in Brazil?' The commissioner, not-so-jokingly, replied, 'Ask a police officer', and said he was tempted to create a panel composed entirely of police officers.

A chilling admission. Black is the dehumanised, the hunted, the useless, the criminalised, the poor in the structure of a racist state.

Reversing economic oppression exposes one of the origins of racism — a very basic assertion that there is not enough to go around, resulting in the belief that some must have less than others.

Why does race exist? To do the accounting for who will have more and who will have less. Race-making takes place even within groups of people with the same skin colour. In South Africa, in 2008, migrants from Mozambique, Malawi and Zimbabwe were killed by black South Africans in riots. And in 2015 and 2017, poor blacks violently attacked people in the Nigerian community, beating and murdering some of them, and burning their homes and shops, in anti-immigration riots. Difference and othering can be marked in many ways — the us versus them of a religion, of geographical territory, or of an ethnicity.

In 1994, the Rwandan genocide was swift and brutal, beginning on 6 April and ending on 19 July. During those months, the murder rate surpassed that of the Nazis in the Holocaust and the Khmer Rouge in the Killing Fields. In about a hundred days, approximately 850,000 individuals were murdered, at a rate of about three-hundred deaths per hour, five deaths per minute. Hutu perpetrators came from all levels of society. Using machetes, swords, spears and nail-studded clubs, Hutu citizens and paramilitaries murdered their Tutsi neighbours, Tutsi wives, Tutsi students, Tutsi patients and fellow Hutus who were considered Tutsi collaborators.

Why? How does race work among kin?

The causes and motives behind the Rwandan genocide are complex, contested, and rooted in a difficult history between the two groups, but one theory[3] explores the fact that prior to the colonisation of Rwanda in the late 1880s by Germany, Belgium and the British, the Hutus and Tutsis lived relatively harmoniously. Through structural inequalities instituted under Belgian governance and in the Catholic school system, Tutsis gained more power, more access to education, and inevitably became the elite in Rwanda. Segregation ensued, with identity cards being introduced in 1933 and identities of *otherness* entrenched in what was once a more fluidly diverse society. During the post-colonial period in the late 1950s, political parties formed along ethnic lines in a similar way as they did in British Guiana, when blacks and Indians began to be represented by different political groups. In 1959, Hutus overthrew the Tutsi monarchy and violent battles between the two groups began. In post-independence Rwanda, Hutus began to discriminate against Tutsis, forcing hundreds of thousands to flee the country. A group of Tutsi exiles formed the Rwandan Patriotic Front and invaded Rwanda in 1990. The violence between the groups escalated.

The willingness of Hutus to slaughter their Tutsi neighbours and vice versa might rest in the roots of racism — that need for some to have more than others based on constructed difference. The economic crisis of 1984, in which food production decreased, the price of coffee crashed and jobs were eliminated, caused hardship for many families. For nearly a decade this crisis fed into the hopelessness felt by many young people, and this hopelessness fed their participation in the genocide in which race-making fuelled the blood-letting. Here as elsewhere, race becomes an economic construct that governs who gets 'more'.

At the heart of othering is fear. 'Whiteness' fears its shadow. We fear that the other will take what we have; in the extreme, this fear becomes hate for the sake of hate, a racialised sadism that strips our humanity.

Class and race are inseparable tools for othering. Slowly over the last two decades of living in London I've seen them in action in ways that, in my middle-class upbringing in Canada, I had not so acutely tracked. When I was a child, my grandmother and I used to watch *To Sir, with Love*, starring Sidney Poitier, every time it came on television. My grandmother would sit through the opening scenes with her hands pressed together in front of her chest, waiting for the moment when 'Sir' (Sidney Poitier) announces that he is from British Guiana. Then she would clap her hands in glee at hearing her birthplace announced on television. I remember once asking her what she thought of the way the teacher in the story was treated by the east London teenagers. She shook her head with a kind of hopelessness, indicating how appalling racism must be in England, blind to her own internalised hierarchy of shades expressed when she instructed me to not 'go backwards' with a black boyfriend. At the end of the film, she said, 'You know, when the black people get into power, they will be just as bad as the white people.' I didn't understand what she meant then, but the statement stayed with me. She knew about elites; she understood that oppression would always come when some had much more than others.

And she ran.

When I first moved to London, I met John Berger and we became friends. We would talk about art and politics in a way that I had never considered possible; he shone light on a kind of socialism that had art at its core. His Marxism seemed different to that of other activists. His writing was so human and humane, so full of a collective longing for beauty that his politics seemed simple, fundamental to the human spirit — obvious. Race-making was class making, and inequality happened as soon as there was an us and a them. In that moment, Berger said, 'barbarism' ensued. He encouraged me to read many authors, among them Arundhati Roy, not only her novel, *The God of Small Things,* but her political essays, all of which contained a meta-physical solidarity among people that straightforward socialist polit-ical writing was often too rigid to admit. In *The God of Small Things* I found ambiguity and mystery — 'The sea was black, the spume vomit green. Fish fed on shattered glass. Night's elbows rested on the water, and falling stars glanced off its brittle shards. Moths lit up the sky. There wasn't a moon.' — and a story of love that straddles caste. In that love there is tragedy, because in the Hindu caste system love relationships between 'untouchables' and higher castes is forbidden. The novel is skilfully unwieldly, perhaps like the southern Indian society it describes. The plot spirals around two deaths, one of a young foreign girl and the other of Velutha, the male lover in the 'illicit' relationship, the God of Small Things himself. I read this novel without putting it down, in awe of Roy's use of language, her fine ear attuned to tiny moments of individual voice, yet able to capture the symphony of a region; hers was an omniscience that knew that small things are the true things, the best things, the only things upon which to make sense of human struggles.

> *If he touched her, he couldn't talk to her, if he loved her he couldn't leave, if he spoke he couldn't listen, if he fought he couldn't win.*
>
> Who was he, the one-armed man? Who could he have been? The God of Loss? The God of Small Things? The God of Goose Bumps and Sudden Smiles? Of Sourmetal Smells — like steel bus-rails and the smell of the bus conductor's hands from holding them?

In this novel, I came into imaginary contact with something that felt familiar from generations ago, from lives and ancestors long gone, but which made sense to my present desire for divisions to collapse. I claimed the 'God of Loss' — whom I had been born to appease, being the replacement child.

I am able to imagine my Indian ancestor as a woman standing beside a river knowing its force, fully aware that in harnessing it something powerful will come. She knows equally that strangling a river to make hydroelectricity will be dangerous in ways she cannot see in this moment. She turns to gather the stories of those living along its shore instead.

Berger and Roy gave me a different way of seeing in which caste and class and the history of inequalities became part of my perceptions of my racialised self. Along with my desire to write towards the skinless, fleshless moment when all the bones danced, I recognised that the racialised liberalism in which I was educated — where we strive for a bigger part of some mythological pie that our fractured identities are in competition for — leaves us without a language with which to talk about inequality. It leaves black and white in perpetual opposition, a state that feeds the plantation mentality.

There is a skin condition called dermatographia, in which faint scratches on the skin redden and rise in a wheal similar to hives. Such skin can be written upon like paper, though the marks disappear after thirty minutes. For a brief moment, the skin is a book, is a record of touch. To touch is to love. To write is also to love.

To answer 'writer' when I'm asked what race I am is true not because I want to avoid the issue of race, but because I want the questioner to think about why I need to be your brown girl in the ring. I am not your yellow lotus, your angry black woman, your Pocahontas. What happens on your skin? What happens to you when you are touched?

Skin affected by dermatographia can be written on, the
writing remaining only briefly, like disappearing ink on paper.
Source: R1carver, Creative Commons.

8

Blood

A desperate foolishness. The crops failed.
I sold my children.

Did my Scottish great-great-great grandmother consider her bloodline? On her deathbed, where I imagine her, does she think about her sons? Her nephews? The book she has been reading tips back in her hands. Sir Walter Scott's *Ivanhoe* has gripped her as much as her chest cough these past few days, and now, at the height of a tournament, with Ivanhoe wounded in the joust and Rebecca tending to him on the ground, and just as an archer splits a willow reed with an arrow, her breathing becomes laboured. There has been no news from her second-born son in Demerara, living among all the brown women, and no one dare tell her the news from New Amsterdam. She is renowned for her weak and, most would say, good heart. Her sons are her pride and joy. Her flesh and blood. She has no idea that her nephews will hang by the neck for murder.

Blood brothers, in the blood, to sign your name in blood, in cold blood, bad blood, blue blood, blood feuds, blood on your hands, blood and thunder: our relationship to blood is pervasive in language, in symbols, in fear and horror, in blood baths as societies oppose one another. Blood runs through us and warms us. In my anger over inequality I have become more and more hot blooded. Perhaps this is progress.

To progress, to learn from history and become more humane: surely this is possible. But what if 'progress' itself is an instrument that divides us? The ideas behind social Darwinism suggest that survival is for the fittest, but who does 'fittest' include? Does one individual progress more effectively than another? Perhaps there is no slow progress towards a more harmonious way of living on the planet. Maybe we go backwards. I don't know. But John Berger says, 'Hope is not a form of guarantee; it's a form of energy, and very frequently that energy is strongest in circumstances that are very dark.'

Evolution, in a purely Darwinian analysis, relies on competition and the slow, agonising struggle to survive in the face of lack or want, what an organism doesn't have. Instead of social evolution, perhaps there is a way to see progress as more lateral: I went from being an unhappy oversensitive child to a relatively content oversensitive adult. I am a product of my porous nature and perhaps any evolution I sense is a result of understanding the primacy of my feelings.

The Chinese and Japanese system of blood groups aligns personality with blood types in storytelling similar to occult interpretation of physiognomy. My blood type is O-negative. In the Chinese system, this means I need to eat meat to sustain my strength. My type defines me as ambitious, confident, intuitive, athletic, but also unpredictably spiteful, cold, ruthless. Of course, I object. Like early physiognomy, this blood-type personality theory has been used in prejudicial pseudo-science. In 1927, Takeji Furukawa, the author of 'The Study of Temperament Through Blood Type', compared the blood types of the indigenous people of Japan and Taiwan in order to 'penetrate the essence of the racial traits of the Taiwanese who recently revolted and behaved so cruelly'. Type O was a big factor in their genetic make-up, and as a result Furukawa concluded that Taiwanese were genetically rebellious. While I like the idea of being genetically rebellious, I no longer accept being told what I am.

If we add the Rh negative factor to the mix, my blood type describes further potential stories. O-negative is a relatively rare configuration of antigens (molecules that can trigger an immune response) and antibodies (molecules that fight antigens). O blood has no antigens but it has antibodies to A and B type blood (it fights their antigens off). The negative factor means that the blood cannot fight off Rh antigens.

Only 6.6 per cent of the population has O-negative blood. Those with O-negative blood are useful in emergencies, universal donors. Trauma and accident victims can have an immediate blood transfusion with our help. It's the safest blood for newborns in need, especially those with underdeveloped immune systems. However, someone with O-negative blood doesn't have the antigens A, B and Rh, and therefore can only accept O-negative blood in a transfusion. The blood system could allow me to create a story of myself: I can give to others, but I can't let others in. I no longer accept this old story of belonging I've been telling myself. I prefer something more complex and poetic.

'Poetry is not a luxury,' says Audre Lorde in *The Master's Tools Will Never Dismantle the Master's House*. A simple truth. She reminds us that there are ways of living that don't require us to feel we need to solve a problem. What are the tools of the Master's House? Phoney 'scientific' reasoning, definitions of otherness, the physiognomy and taxonomy of humans in the age of so-called Enlightenment. These ideas freed some people and enslaved others. We can't rely solely upon our ideas to make us free. Lorde says instead we can respect our feelings, 'those hidden sources of our power from where true knowledge and, therefore, lasting action comes'. Instead of 'I think, therefore I am', in order to be free, Lorde encourages me to listen to the whispers in my dreams, to be aware of feeling too.

Poetry can be revolutionary after all. 'Rise like lions after slumber' Shelley tells us, and Allen Ginsberg pleads with us in *Howl* to remember the 'supernatural extra brilliant intelligent kindness of the soul'. If we pay attention to language and its power — if we understand that shame buries our anger but also our compassion, and makes us retreat from one another — there is a way forward. A new path.

Our mixed blood.

As a child and teenager and even into my twenties, I secretly believed that if everyone was like me, truly racially mixed, we wouldn't be mixed up — there couldn't possibly be racism. Like the man at Speakers' Corner in Hyde Park in 1956, I felt that the end of racism was an evolutionary project. When people realised that we are all so much alike, that 'purity' did not exist, we'd all be finally free.

In fact, all people are already mixed — we are all cousins. The lines that have been drawn between us have nothing to do with biology.

Black blood, white blood, brown blood, yellow blood, red blood. Mixed blood. In the nineteenth century, Darwin still believed that blood was the agent of inheritance. Blood, semen, fluids — things that were liquid and could easily become mixed with one another — were seen by the ancient Greeks as containing the essence of an individual. Pythagoras first suggested that human life begins with a mix of male and female fluids. Into this story of inheritance comes the rights associated with it. The blood of kings, blue blood, royal blood, passed through bloodlines and birthright, whether to a nation state or a family. The idea of liquids mixing has also been used in controlling who is identified as what, for example in the 'one drop' rule in the United States, which was used to enlarge the slave population by categorising the illegitimate children of slave holders.

In Canada, the Indian Act, first passed in 1876, set out the rights promised to First Nations people by the British King George III. It defines who is recognised as 'Indian' — who has 'status' and who does not. It has also been used to discriminate along gender lines and to mandate forced education — practices that the country's recent Truth and Reconciliation Commission called cultural genocide. *The blood of others.*

The yellow badges that Jews were required to wear in Nazi Germany are a potent example of how fearful people in power use symbols of otherness to define race. But the logic of bloodlines, of tracing heritage and inheritance through blood, and now through genes, breaks down in the face of atavism — when an individual trait from a previous generation shows up in a child who looks nothing like her parents. There the story of 'blending liquids' is challenged.

In my extended family of mixed Guyanese people, traits are not 'blended' at all — a nose is not a partially diluted African or 'Caucasian' nose, but shows up in its entirety in different, often unexpected places: a blond child of two brown parents, the almond-shaped eyes of one sibling and the round eyes and flat, broad nose of her sister.

As we know now, inheritance is not in the blood but in the genes, which are distinct physical units passed on through sperm and egg. But the emphasis on mixing is still omnipresent in stories around race today. The idea that it's *all in the genes* — our health, destiny, future and history — is similar to the preoccupation with blood, one drop of it. From the discoveries based on garden peas by Gregor Mendel in 1860s, to the Human Genome Project, which is attempting to map the entire genetic make-up of the human species through time, our desire to understand just *what* we are persists. But perhaps genetics will yield a different kind of narrative that remains humane rather than divisive. As the statement from the National Human Genome Research Institute reveals, the project has a basis in storytelling:

> [The genome] is a history book — a narrative of the journey of our species through time. It's a shop manual, with an incredibly detailed blueprint for building every human cell. And it's a transformative textbook of medicine, with insights that will give health care providers immense new powers to treat, prevent and cure disease.[1]

Historical views of mixed races, mixed bloods, half-bloods were infected by the same ideas that supported slavery. Language associated with animals — for example, the word *mulatto*, the sterile mule — was also used to underscore the fear of boundaries between races being broken down and to continue the racist project of white supremacy.

In 1883, Edward Gilliam wrote an influential essay that appeared in *Popular Science Monthly*, noting with concern that in the United States the 'Negro' population was growing faster than the white population. The next year, in an essay entitled 'The African Problem', he suggested that the lack of social integration after the abolition of slavery was a natural, biological phenomenon, because 'white repugnance [at fusion] has a scientific and permanent basis'. He believed that, based on the prevailing notions around brain size, mulattoes who were predominantly white would be almost as intelligent as whites. But those who were only a quarter or an eighth white would be less intelligent than pure blacks. This promise of increasing inferiority as a result of 'mixing' was used as a deterrent to interracial relations. Horror movies, the gothic fears of crossed boundaries, Jane Eyre's first sighting of Bertha Mason, the idea that impurities are dangerous: these stories serve a purpose in race-making.

However, in plant biology, the offspring of a cross between different genotypes is often more vigorous than its parents. 'Hybrid vigour' manifests in many ways, including rate of growth, early flowering, increased yield. Hybrid corn is meant to be the sweetest. The vigour of hybridity, of crossing boundaries, is what we all have, already.

Crossing boundaries is what migrants do, what refugees do. The outcome is new for all involved, both for those who travel and for those who remain. There is loss and gain. Colonisers also cross boundaries, but real hybridity is not possible in a colonial state, as hybridity defies hierarchy.

My childhood notion of harmony for the world hasn't come to fruition — and still seems impossible in a world that perpetually chooses racism, anti-blackness, islamophobia, misogyny, homophobia, white supremacy, extremist nationalism and many other forms of hatred. But I still see hybridity as a creative tool, a way of focussing new thoughts and actions. East, west, north, south intersecting; the oral and written entwining; genres overlapping: all to show off our complexity. I believe there is a way to stop othering nature, too — *Trees are who and not what.* I am at home among the displaced. I can make a virtue out of my lack of belonging.

In Mabaruma this past Easter, I read a *Guyana Chronicle* article headlined, 'Mabaruma Police Assaulted by Baccoo'. A baccoo is a Guyanese spirit who engages in mysterious activities for purposes of revenge and theft. Likely derived from a Yoruba spirit called Abiku, a baccoo is a short man with large eyes, long arms and legs without kneecaps who pelts houses with stones, moves objects several times its weight, and lives on bananas and milk. The article reported that strange occurrences had been taking place in the Mabaruma settlement, including a girl 'possessed' who demonstrated inhuman strength, an inexplicable rain of bricks upon the police station and the disappearance of chickens, who left their feathers behind. As we waited for our flight back to Georgetown, my cousins and I decided to approach a local police officer to ask him about the story. He told us he had encountered many baccoo in his short life, and had even been thrown across a room. He believed that the young girl had been possessed, because she had flung the colleague who tried to deal with her out of the house.

The story of the baccoo came to me out of the blue of the past, out of the history of a Yoruba statue of Abiku that must have come to Guyana with an enslaved Nigerian. The slave stories lamented the death of a child still unnamed, who would be called upon to enact small acts of rebellion through magic. The stories were shared over and over with others on a plantation, shared with those who came after abolition, repeated and transformed like a game of broken telephone over generations of Guyanese people to make sense of the inexplicable. It reminds me of all the stories my mother told me throughout my life that I don't know how to verify, and it reminds me that storytelling is hybridity itself, and that stories can change, be forgotten, be replaced.

Caryl Phillips' *Crossing The River* is a novel that crosses boundaries of time and place; it mixes voices and histories; characters leave home and find home. It is a story that begins in shame, with the father of three children lamenting his 'desperate foolishness'. Two simple sentences capture the history of the African diaspora in a devastating snapshot: 'The crops failed. I sold my children'. He mourns, 'My Nash. My Martha. My Travis'. But these children are related over centuries; they are only siblings in the sense that they are products of the African diaspora, displaced by slavery. Nash is the African child sold to slave-traders by his father and eventually freed by another 'father', his white master, to live in Liberia. Martha, who is separated from her husband and daughter at a slave auction, is determined not to die in bondage in Kansas, and runs away, crossing the Missouri River in an attempt to reach free California. Travis, centuries later, is an American GI in the Second World War, who finds himself in England and falls in love with Joyce, a married Englishwoman, with whom he has a child. Prominent in the novel is the pained voice of a white slave-trader, Captain Hamilton, who conceals his participation in the slave trade, sanitising it his passionate letters to his wife as the business of commodity trading. The legacies of slavery and war eventually bring the mixed-race child of Travis and Joyce back to England in search of understanding. The novel retraces the steps of ancestors as they cross borders, mental and psychological spaces, in order to make meaning out of fractured selves. The journeys are poetic and heart-breaking: the leg irons, the oceans and rivers, the people huddling together, 'the many tongued chorus of the common memory' of people who have been forced into servitude and, yes, the shame of that original ancestor who sold his child.

The work of words is a country to belong to.

As I pack my suitcase, I am nervous. Every summer before I head back to Canada to visit my family and friends, I'm hit with anxiety. This time I realise I'm afraid of seeing my mother diminished — and also afraid of the mirror she will provide for my own inevitable decline.

In London the heat has not let up. And elsewhere, cars have turned to molten metal on Greek roads as wildfires wipe small villages off the map. A newspaper headline tells me that the death toll is as high as eighty, in the 'biblical disaster' that is sweeping the countryside in the region of Rafina, where the town of Mati has been devastated. Wind and lightning, fire and brimstone. Another newspaper headline predicts the draining of the Lake District in England as Britain scrambles for water. Hospital patients in London are passing out and vomiting owing to the extreme temperatures. Viruses. The threat of plague.

Although I long for the lake at my sister's cottage, I am also afraid of what I am leaving behind in Europe — that important things, dangerous things, will go on while I'm gone. That my loved ones here will be harmed somehow, that people or dreams will die. The grip of the heat, the bad faith of current politics, the slow burning end-of-times feel in the long hot days, the sleepless nights, unsettle me to the point of wanting to run away and simultaneously hold tight to my kitchen counter.

I arrive in Toronto to cooler temperatures. As I sit with my mother in the living room of her small house in the east end, the heat is bearable. She wears a sleeveless dress and I see that her arms are reduced to sinews, the bones frail, but her face is bright, and she looks still beautiful. There are moments when her face shocks me with its youth — eternal, painful in its innocence. We walk to a local Greek restaurant and have lunch. She eats heartily, and tells me about her neighbours, friends who keep an eye out for her. I tell her about my writing and that I would like more stories from her. She tilts her head and looks at the stucco ceiling above a portrait of a nymph, as though for inspiration. She shakes her head. She doesn't have anything for me, and I feel cruel for even asking her. She's more concerned about when we are leaving for the cottage, and how many days we'll stay.

As we walk home, she holds on to to my arm, and when I ask her if she's okay she assures me that of course she is; she makes this walk all the time. But she's breathing heavily, so I slow down. Every few minutes she points at the trees, remarking on how beautiful they are. 'Oh, look at that,' she says, straining to breathe, 'and that one!' I wonder if she's trying to distract me from her breathlessness, or whether, truly, she finds real excitement in the beauty and majesty of the trees.

The next day we leave in my rented car for my sister's cottage on Shadow Lake. On the highway we crawl slowly northward in heavy traffic. We talk about family casually, catching up on the latest events in the lives of my nieces and nephews, and she asks me again how long we'll be at the cottage and when we'll go back home and how she'll get there.

———

I stand on the dock, the lake before me, inviting, and yet I am aware of the spot near the island where my foot felt that first brush with the fishing lure. Spruce, white birch and tall pine trees make dancing shadows on the rocks near the shore. I dive into the lake and swim, feeling my entire body as it pushes through water. I float on my back and look up at the sky to see if it's the same sky as in the tropics, the same sheltering blue I felt in Barbados. A heron passes over and I gasp. It has come so close it's clear it does not consider me a concern.

As I float, I remember childhood summers at friends' cottages and a boy named Jim. Late one night, he and I swam out into a different lake, not far from here, with a gang of other kids. I remember the feeling of sinking while all the others glided towards the floating dock. I tried to keep up with Jim. I couldn't, but when we all got there, I was the first to pull myself up on the dock, showing that I could at least leap onto cold, wet wood. On the dock we sat and told jokes and played truth or dare, and I wished for a dare that involved Jim, but I never got it.

I turn over and swim back to the shore.

My brother's children, all in their twenties, have an Irish mother; my sister's children, teenagers, are adopted, mixed-race boys, one with a Ghanaian father and English-Canadian mother, the other with Guyanese parents of mixed heritage. I believe that none of them has spent much time dealing with race as an issue: they are from a different, more fluid generation, and they are all relatively wealthy — miles away from being black bodies on urban streets, from being stopped and searched or carded by the police. But when I ask them some questions, I'm surprised by how much space race has taken up in their lives.

My brother's children are fair-skinned, barely golden-brown at the height of the summer. Raised on a farm near a relatively small town, they tell me that they were the odd ones out at their school. My youngest niece has wild, thick, tight curls that she has tamed in response to being the only black girl at an all-white high school. My eldest nephew is tall and lanky, big-boned, Viking-like, but with a face much like my Chinese grandmother's. As I listen, I catch myself thinking in these ethnic terms and feel ashamed.

I have assigned body parts to regional definitions, and I am in the same trap of genes and ethnicity that I want others to escape.

My nephew is a man now, with a doctorate in Human Anatomy Education, but I will never forget him as a very young boy on one particular Thanksgiving as we shovelled in turkey and stuffing. In the middle of a heated family discussion about race, I turned to him as he sat innocently playing with a few Lego pieces at his place, and said: 'What colour are you, then?' He looked up at me and gave the question his deepest respect and consideration. After many seconds he had the answer: 'Blue, I guess.'

Now he tells me that the biggest problem he has with race is not that no one knows 'what' he is, but that in conversations that are clearly racist among acquaintances, he is brought into the fold as I once was, exempt from consideration — 'But not you, no, not you.'

My eldest niece looks the most Chinese of the three, showing how genetics is not a blending of inks, in which yellow and white become beige. She has more easily engaged in conversations around race, ethnicity and othering, which she understands through the demands of her social work training and her community-based work. She tells me she was once asked to be a part of a celebration of south Asian women; this puzzled her because she in no way looks south Asian. She wonders if just one othering is enough to allow her into all spaces of the 'other'. These three young people live in the shadow of whiteness, their own and the society's in which they live, but they have a private, nearly secret, awareness of the complexity of their background, without a new language to account for it.

My sister's children are still both in high school. They are the two with the darkest skin and the most clearly racialised features.

The younger one, slouched in the armchair, stares at his phone, while the older one, known for his sensitivity and guilelessness, pays attention beside me on the couch. He was once called the N-word by one white boy in school, he says. I brace myself for his rage or his hurt feelings, and am surprised when he tells me that his response was to stand in front of the boy and say, 'So what?' And to attempt to defuse the boy's racism by telling him that he was way behind the times — that his mother had been called that long ago as a teenager. I get choked up at his reaction to racism as out of fashion. I let him continue. The fact that he remembers a specific event from his mother's stories about her youth, and uses this story as a defence against a verbal assault, moves me. He adds that the boy was expelled from school after being reported by another classmate. Another boy called him the N-word but that boy was black. He barely differentiates the two situations of the N-word: merely a word that he now associates with something that he shares with his mother.

I ask his brother if he's ever experienced racism and he — not a big talker, and the youngest among us — shakes his head, still intent on his phone. I know that this might be true, but I try to draw him out.

'What is race?' I say.

He shrugs.

'Okay, what race are you?'

He looks at me briefly, then back at his phone, and shrugs again. I feel guilty, forcing him to think about something he hasn't had to consider. When his brother prods him for an answer, he says 'Everything.'

I am humbled. I ask them if they ever feel like they don't belong. They both answer with a firm *No*. My sister looks at me, pointedly, and I decide to ask one more question and leave it at that.

'When you're up here, at the cottage, and we go into the Foodland and people stare at us, do you feel different?'

'He does now that you've suggested it,' my sister says, and I am stung by her tone. The younger one only shrugs again and the older one says, 'I don't care if they're staring ... we're outsiders we're not locals — they don't see us every day.' Once again a child has humbled me. Belonging is what you give yourself, and he has plenty. He is not like I was at his age, and for this I am grateful.

But these are not the young boys who are carded, who are racially profiled while walking down the street in Toronto, who are shot for being black. I racialised them in our conversation, while all along their socio-economic status shelters them from the harsher realities of bodies in trouble.

Later in the afternoon, my mother and sister decide they need some groceries. My sister brings the car round and I watch my mother approach the stairs that lead from the porch to where the car waits for her. As I'm thinking it, it happens — her right foot flies out in front of her and she slips but catches the railing just in time, holding tight.

My heart stops rather than races, as I rush towards her.

She's fine, she's fine, she assures me and although I see that she is, I am shaking. She takes deep breaths, winces and shakes out her knee, and continues to walk towards the car. I can only marvel. She and my sister head off, while I sit in the shade and wait for them, blaming the heat for her fall, managing to blame climate change for the slippery stairs, blaming myself for living so far away.

My mother will die one day, and I cannot blame the plantation for that. I can only hope that *Oh, the world* might be more gentle before she does.

My visit to the lake coincides with two anniversaries: the death of my father and the fishing lure accident. The sound of my father's voice, the smell of the nursing home, the fear in his eyes, that single hour of real pain before he was given relief, and his last word on the planet, which I keep to myself, a secret between us, but which I perform as he asked me to, silently, every day. Every day. These things visit me in the night, as I sleep in the same bed I did with my sister the day after he died, which neither of us left for nearly twenty-four hours after. It's a difficult night and I have uncomfortable dreams. Loons call to one another on the lake.

I think I smell smoke.

There are wildfires burning not far from here, on the other side of the Trans-Canada Highway: the main thoroughfare towards the big water — Georgian Bay, Lake Huron, and beyond them the biggest of the Great Lakes, Lake Superior. Some of the fires are out of control. There has been no rain. Evacuation warnings are in place. I remember childhood summers on lakes, camping, the taste of burnt marshmallows, a hot dog skewered along its entire length with care by my father, while I took care not to mention his veterinary skill with dogs, for fear that it would be a bad joke. The stick would be barely long enough to reach the flames, and I would feel the smoke in my throat. The wind would change and the smoke would drift in the opposite direction for a few minutes of relief, hitting my brother, sister or cousins on the other side. I would hold tight to George the monkey while adults told stories around the fire.

There are fires in so many places across Canada — Kamloops, Snowy Mountain, Whitetail Creek, all in British Columbia. And also Saddleworth Moor in England, Yosemite Valley in California, Kineta, Greece, Potsdam, Germany, Karbole, Sweden. And here in bed at the lake I wonder if this is what the world will taste like now. A perpetual campfire.

Everything is uncomfortable and urgent. My father's last word. My mother's grasp of the days. A plantation igniting. I remember that somewhere in the tropics sugar cane is burning before the harvest.

The loons call out again.

I wonder what amends I thought I had to make to the different parts of myself in feeling the shame of race. What my whiteness, blackness, yellowness and indigeneity have to do with one another. I wonder what kind of statement I need to make for my nieces and nephews on the history of their family or if they are already making those connections much faster than I ever did. What I know is that they need to make their lives a fully embodied, meaningful quest for their own authenticity, and they must avoid the greed that creates race, the lie of 'success'.

I get angry, because I have access to anger now, and am no longer a woman who defaults to sadness. The plantation is every-where. The crops are no longer merely sugar or cotton but a host of sugar-like products, mass-produced and cheap to buy, yielding huge profits for their owners and investors in corporations reliant on cheap labour.

Cheap living. Cheap lives. Throughout the history of sugar

production, cheap sugar and cheap labour have been entwined. During the run-up to the abolition of slavery in the British colonies in 1833, planters raised alarm over the rising price of production should they actually have to pay for the labour required to harvest and refine sugar cane. The association of planters started petitions claiming that abolition would be the ruin of the empire. They sent these to the government to lobby for the status quo:

> If abolition, unconditional, unqualified abolition shall
> take place, our interest in the West-India islands must
> be at an end ... the revenue will suffer an annual
> diminution of three millions at least: the price of
> sugar, which is now become a necessary article of life,
> must be immediately enhanced; discontentment and
> dissatisfaction may dismember the empire ...[2]

After abolition, the sugar market did suffer a blow. British sugar produced by free labour at higher prices couldn't compete with sugar produced by slave labour in Cuba and Brazil. The British government brought in tax reforms on imports of sugar under the Sugar Duties Act of 1846, and these had a devastating effect on the economies of the plantations in the Caribbean, which had previously enjoyed reduced import duties. Sugar from beetroot in Europe became a cheap alternative to cane sugar. The crop that once created nations in the Caribbean lost ground to cheaper competitors. The people who had been transported there, who worked the land, built the society around the crop and raised their children as British subjects, saw the industry abandoned because it was no longer profitable.

The profit motive requires producers to expand the reach of products, producing cheap things at the cheapest rate based on the cheapest labour. Cheap clothes, so we all look the same. The same but not equal. Cheap food, cheap energy, cheap care, cheap technology, cheap pharmaceuticals. The product itself does not define the plantation. It is defined by its structure and the labour done by the people upon which its cheap products rely.

Poster decrying the false economy of cheap sugar.
Source: British Library.

My eldest niece saw her otherness as aligned with every othered group in society. In this alignment perhaps there is resistance. What are we resisting? *Oh, the world* — the pain and suffering for others. We are resisting a state of mind that says there's not enough for us all, because I need more than I have — or at least more than you. But we are also resisting the state of mind that refuses to put each other and the planet first.

'Hope,' says John Berger, 'is an act of faith and has to be sustained by other concrete actions ... The act of resistance means not only refusing to accept the absurdity of the world-picture offered us, but denouncing it. And when hell is denounced from within, it ceases to be hell.'

The main thing I want to tell the young people in my life around race is that the reparations my white self needs to make to my black and indigenous self are not about race at all. The reparations have to do with taking action. Now. In shelving my obedience to a liberal system that says that success is made on the backs of others, while state-sponsored violence theoretically keeps me 'free'. That is not freedom. The main message for my 'blood' relations is that their responsibility to themselves mirrors their responsibilities to others, and that everyone must engage in the humility it takes to repair our relations with each other and the planet. Radical, mutual care, starting now.

I think of a quote from Angela Davis: 'You have to act as if it were possible to radically transform the world. And you have to do it all the time.'

The wind has changed direction; I no longer smell smoke. I hope I will get some sleep.

FINDINGS

Double Helix

I saw a high hill and on it a form
shaped against hard air.

It could have been just a pole with
some old cloth attached,

but as I came closer

I saw it was a human body

The grass in Kensington Gardens is tawny and dry, yet people still lie out on green and white striped canvas lounge chairs as though on England's green and pleasant land.

A roller-blader and some cyclists pass in front of me as I walk across the lawn towards the paved avenue that divides the park from Kensington Palace and makes a thoroughfare north and south from Queensway to Kensington High Street. I cross the pavement to get a look at Queen Victoria. I've always been curious about why her statue is so small, much smaller than her husband's nearby gilt bronze figure under its own ornate canopy.

When I got back from Ontario, I found the rosemary, basil and mint in the small herb pot on my terrace dead and shrivelled. The trestle holding my jasmine plant had been toppled by strong winds in a storm at the height of the incomparable heat, and the jasmine plant barely survived. I thought this a sign: I should leave my flat and head back to Toronto where I would be a better daughter to my mother, a better sibling to my brother and sister, a better friend to my lifelong friends there. But I have work to do, a new job, and a new project on loneliness and stories that is a collaboration with other writers and community groups.

My jetlag has subsided and I feel ready to work. Jetlag is our bodies' reminder that we are not supposed to travel that far, that fast. Any kind of travel can be disorienting for a body, but air travel heightens the rupture, displacement, disorientation. *Perdre le nord* (to lose north) is a French phrase that means to lose one's bearings, to lose track of the compass point that guides you. My split life between North America and Europe always includes a moment of losing north on each side of the Atlantic.

I left my mother in Toronto standing on the steps of her small house. Each year when I leave, she promises she won't cry, but she always does. This year we both cried. Her shoulders hunched, her hands over her mouth, she reminded me of a woodland creature clutching a fallen seed, as my taxi drove off towards the airport. Rupture is what migrants, refugees, immigrants and other runaways experience. It's brutal and damaging, necessary and painful. As I remember that my DNA results should be back soon, I am certain that one thing they will fail to track is the pain related to migration.

I doubt any of the DNA evidence will undo the mark on the

eight-year-old me who didn't know how to answer *What Are You?* Identification is not identity. Shared traits do not equal shared identity. My identity has been fluid as I move back and forth across the Atlantic, back and forth between art and institution, between screen and page, between my past and my present. Once I took responsibility for what this 'self' is, and responsibility for my own contentment, facing my shadows and their sources, new questions arose. What action should I take in the world? What responsibilities do I have?

Race is the story of the self told by a stranger, with 'white' as the primordial narrator. If we disable that narrator, new stories based on true identity rather than identification become possible. But what is a true identity? The plantation divides by its very nature. To resist that division is to maintain hope in discovering a true self.

Not far from the statue of Queen Victoria — diminutive compared to her broken likeness in Georgetown — is the blackened skeleton of Grenfell Tower where a flash fire destroyed the 120 homes of the twenty-four-storey block, killing at least seventy-two people. Woken by helicopters circling on that June morning, I went onto my terrace to see smoke billowing from across the city, the tower in my sights as it burned, but I did not know as I stood watching just what was happening — how the smoke that bloated in the early morning sky would clear and reveal public housing unfit for humans, the government's neglect of the poorest people. Cheap combustible cladding was supposed to protect them. The government had authorised companies who knew it was insufficient to install the material in hundreds of social housing buildings across the country, and this cladding still lines towers similar to Grenfell. It is the thin, insufficient skin between poverty and disaster.

The Slavery Abolition Act of 1833 provided for compensation of slave owners whose business would be affected by the lack of free labour. The government of the United Kingdom paid out a total of £20 million, which at the time was forty per cent of its national budget, to buy the freedom of all the slaves in the empire. The slaves themselves never received a single pound of the 'compensation'. The money was such a large percentage of the national budget and the loan to pay it so substantial that the debt was only paid off in 2015. Descendants of slaves in the UK paid for the compensation given to slave owners for nearly two centuries. And towers where the poorest live go up in flames.

I can't breathe.

Fire continues to be everywhere this summer, but even in disaster movies the screenwriter uncovers the humanity. In Helsinki, Finland, temperatures in early August usually average nineteen degrees celsius; now they are a steady thirty degrees. One supermarket owner invited a hundred customers to sleep in his air-conditioned premises at night to beat the heat. In Berlin and Hamburg, police have used water cannons, normally deployed to control riots, to water the parched trees in the city centres. In various communities on a daily basis, people work side by side for the good of that community. Grenfell Tower residents and supporters pushed back against political solutions that offered condolences but no change, and they continue to work to force awareness and political action, to change social housing, to unearth injustices. In London, Praxis works with refugees and migrants to advocate, develop skills, give voice, build community; the Limehouse Project seeks to empower marginalised individuals in the borough of Tower Hamlets; One Day Without Us advocates for migrant workers. In London, Toronto, New York, Chicago, San Francisco and many other communities across North America and Europe there are growing activist networks that join up the resistance to various urgent social and political trends that hurt communities. These networks work locally but on common causes that are global. Groups like Extinction Rebellion, who are creating networks of action-oriented disobedience in the face of the climate emergency; groups opposing fracking, opposing pipelines that invade indigenous land; opposing corporate buy-outs; opposing, as Surfers Against Sewage do, the destruction of the ocean. La Via Campesina is a coalition of organisations in over eighty countries, which advocates family farm-based sustainable agriculture for food sovereignty. The Wretched of the Earth is a grassroots collective for indigenous, black, brown and diaspora groups and individuals demanding climate justice and acting in solidarity with communities in the UK and the global south. Migrants from the global south are escaping climate disasters. While our towns are burning, theirs are flooded, already submerged.

Toronto's Activist Calendar is packed with events and news of small and large victories. Bridges Not Walls, Queer Solidarity

Smashes Borders, Unite Against Islamophobia: the placards on protests across Europe and North America say everything about how organising might be the only way forward. These issues are at the centre of what race is, and they can be joined up.

Joining up is important, because the plantation is a lonely place.

Single-person households are mushrooming; we live our lives online and in the echo chambers of social media. Statistics on loneliness and its prevalence in UK society and elsewhere have raised alarm, with some researchers describing loneliness as a condition with consequences as serious to health as those associated with smoking. In the loneliness project I have been working on, our group of researchers have differing views from the disease model, with some insisting on a place for solitude in our lives, but most agree that loneliness is something that we must take stock of in our noisy, crowded disenfranchised daily lives.

A particle physicist who is part of our group tried to explain string theory to me, and said, with a wave of his hand from my head down to my feet, 'You're a symphony.' I thought he was referring to my specific multi-racial genetic complexity, and possibly even to the song of sugar that forms me, but then he immediately turned to my co-director, a white male, and waved his hand at him in an identical fashion, top to bottom. 'And you're standing beside another symphony.'

He explained that all matter is made up of particles that vibrate at different frequencies to form various shapes and colours, all responses to light. The vibrations in every object in our universe are co-dependent, necessarily harmonious; yet as human beings, we are ultimately alone in a vast cosmos. I deal with human stories as a way to bridge gaps between people. When we read we are not alone. When we resist we are not alone. New stories offer new ways of seeing. Community action, art and activism are paths towards new spaces beyond the plantation — a place outside both the master's house and the field. It is the place I imagine my grandmother now runs to, and stays — a place of her own making, free, and among others who are equally free.

As a child, when I read 'is-land' for island I was thrown into the mystery of language and how it works, how it is invented and gains meaning. Like the word Negro in our schoolbook — a new word that none in the class knew — words are learned in context, and they have power and possibility. They have history and intention. It's possible that I am — you are — only a product of all the words we have ever believed in. I imagine that there is a way forward in which Marx, Jung, Buddha, Malcolm X, Walter Rodney, Martin Luther King Jr., Frantz Fanon, Audre Lorde, Angela Davis, James Baldwin, Stuart Hall, The Standing Rock Sioux Tribe, Families of Sisters in Spirit, Idle No More, the Black Panthers, Greenpeace, Black Lives Matter, Stonewall, Momentum, Occupy, Extinction Rebellion and particle physicists are all elements of a new poetry that seeks to liberate us.

Poetry has no borders. Its horizons are within us.

What if in your previous life
You were born a black man's camera?

———

I love this body
made to weather the storm
in the brain, raised
out of the deep smell
of fish & water hyacinth
out of rapture & the first
regret.

———

The sharp knife of dawn glitters in my hand ...

———

Yes, here's a room
so warm & blood-close,
I swear, you will wake —
& mistake these walls
for skin.

———

someone will find us brittle-winged
beyond the punishments of leaves, of docile trees
of windows, of our own skeletons

My eyes are always hungry.

The wind
was cleansing the bones
They stood forth silver and necessary.

I am the cinnamon
peeler's wife. Smell me.

These are puzzles of language and meaning to sit with, sleep under, see into. In these poets — in order, Terrance Hayes, Yusef Komunyakaa, Martin Carter, Ocean Vuong, Dionne Brand, Audre Lorde, Anne Carson, Michael Ondaatje — I find parts of that ragged self of childhood but also myself in the present. Poetry defies time, is uncontainable, noisy, silent and active; it gives space, allows connection but also solitude; it is all the words that are possible in all the formulations imaginable. Poetry is infectious. I am formed of the reading I have done throughout my life, and from poetry: of toil, of sugar, salt, oil, wheat, cotton, tobacco, corn, tar, feathers, silk, rice, leather, dung and flies. From all those women with their hands in soil.

Every time I read Anne Carson's few words on justice I am re-immersed in the simple complexity of life:

On the day He was to create justice
God got involved in making a dragonfly
and lost track of time.

Like particle physics and string theory, there are different stories
rooted in science that explain what we are. In one — infectious
heredity — we are not the slow, incremental sum of mutations
over millennia, but are being constantly changed by the viruses and
bacteria that pass between our bodies. In this theory, based on the
microbiological research of Carl Woese, whose work challenged
Darwin's origin of life theory and introduced 'horizontal gene
transfer', life began with a very simple collection of cells, and these
cells liked to *share*. They were a 'commune' of cells exchanging
chemicals in order to survive together. In our ancient puddle, let's
say you and I are both cells, and our environment becomes colder,
but you don't get sick, you can handle it, while I'm shivering.
Since our membranes are porous, our genes leak out towards one
another, and I absorb some of yours to allow me to survive the
cold. And now we're both not sick.

Other scientists, extending Woese's work, claim that evolution is an interlude in the real story of life, that the biodiversity
of the planet proliferated until one period three billion years ago
when one strain of bacterium stopped sharing. In this dramatic
moment our cells went from the age of sharing to the age of selfishness. Then came species, difference, slow change. Then came
competition.

And yet in the present, the original sharing between membranes persists. Further scientific studies inform us that when we

are infected with a virus or when we transfer bacteria among us, a little bit of our DNA goes with it, so that in fact we are changing one another on a daily basis. Microbiologists estimate that eight per cent of the human genome is viral DNA, which has come into our systems via bacteria and viruses.

We are in perpetual intimacy.

———

My first set of DNA results arrive, from Ancestry.com, unceremoniously by email on what few people know is the anniversary of the day the transatlantic slave trade was authorised by Charles I, King of Spain: 18 August 1518. Previous to this, slaves had been transported from Africa via the Arab slave trade to Portugal and Spain, and then transported to the Americas. The charter allowed the trade to bypass Europe with 'precious cargo' meant for plantations in the Caribbean. Five hundred years ago on this day, the Spanish king gave one of his top councillors, Lorenzo de Gorrevod, permission to transport 'four thousand negro slaves both male and female' to 'the [West] Indies, the [Caribbean] islands and the [American] mainland of the [Atlantic] ocean sea, already discovered or to be discovered', by ship 'direct from the [West African] isles of Guinea and other regions from which they are wont to bring the said negros'.[1]

The royal document by Charles 1, King of Spain, which launched the transatlantic slave trade in 1518. Source: Ministry of Culture and Sports of the Government of Spain/ Archivo General de Indias.

The email from Ancestry.com describes my body in regions. Some percentages are larger than others — Great Britain, East Asia — and these are not a surprise. The other percentages are small numbers that add up to a majority. Native North American, Scandinavia, Polynesia, Iberian Peninsula, Nigeria, Mali, Senegal, Ivory Coast/ Ghana, Cameroon/ Congo, Europe East, Middle East, Benin/ Togo, Finland/ Northwest Russia, Caucasus — all these little bits of me. How does someone make an identity from them?

While I'm pleased that my DNA bears out family stories, there is one glaring omission in my stats. No mention of South Asian. This can't be true. My father's side of the family, my uncles and cousins, look distinctly Indian. Is it possible that my DNA is closer to my mother's and not my father's and that my sister and brother have different percentages? Genetics do work like that, but I regret the loss of the Indian ancestor I imagined squatting in a rice field in Demerara.

I have travelled to what I thought were parts of myself: Africa, the Caribbean, South America, Southeast Asia, Scotland, many places in Europe, and India twice, most recently the year after my father died. I was told more than once while I was there that I looked like I had ancestors from northeast India, near the border of Bhutan. On long walks in the Himalayan mountains I regularly saw my father in the birds, said hello without hesitation or shyness, and during yoga in the afternoons I came to know my body through my breath, and I understood it very differently to the way I had as a young athlete. Yoga is not about striving, is not like high jumping or running races. It is not about winning or wanting more from the world. It's about balance and letting go, ending up in shavasana, the corpse pose, because that's where we all end up. On a mountain walk, after two weeks of writing in a small Tibetan cabin on a mountain near Dharmsala, I briefly left my body and saw myself from above. What I saw in a flash was me being in the right life, the right body, this child of this father and mother who had lost their first son — here on this planet at this particular time in order to experience it.

My therapist dismissed me from her care a few months later. In Jungian psychoanalytic terms I had passed a threshold of integration that was akin to growing up. Finally.

Fool me once, shame on you; fool me twice, shame on me. I don't want to live on the plantation, take part in it, sow its seeds on this land. I don't need more than I have. I need to make sure that others have what they need. To be part of action, part of a sea change that is urgently needed.

I hold on to the image of my Indian ancestor squatting not because I don't trust the science of DNA, but because it doesn't account for all the songs or symphonies we are, or for literature, or for out of body experiences, for my father in the birds, my mother's awe of the trees, for the perfection of being in the right life, the right body.

Island. Is land. With a silent *s* land can be surrounded by water, and with the addition of a space a question can be formed out of a single word. If we can make new worlds on the page, surely we can bring them into life. Language is like genes, making bodies. Perhaps the imagination is stronger than the body. It certainly outlives it.

A week later, the DNA results from 23&Me are in.

There are distinct overlaps between the findings, which is comforting, but 23&Me has included South Asian as part of my inheritance. It's a small percentage, and perhaps this is why it didn't show up in the Ancestry results. Other percentages and regions are also more detailed than the Ancestry listing, specifying France, Germany, Indonesia, Thailand, Cambodia, Myanmar, Vietnam,

Manchuria and Mongolia, but the Middle Eastern gene is missing. The technology is not foolproof, but like the hundreds of Ancestry cousins that I have, I have over 950 DNA rélatives — third, fourth and fifth cousins — in my 23&Me DNA family.

The analysis informs me that my maternal haplogroup (L) — the migration of women in my maternal line — can be traced back to a single woman who lived in eastern Africa between 150,000 and 200,000 years ago. Another maternal haplogroup (D) can be traced to a common ancestor who lived in Asia nearly 40,000 years ago. And within this group my D4 gene is common among Koreans and the populations of Manchuria. Recent archaeological discoveries suggest that the earliest inhabitants of Korea probably came from the Altai-Sayan and Baikal regions of Southeast Siberia. They likely began to move into the region about 30,000 years ago, when they followed mammoths and other large animals into the peninsula. Among Siberian populations, haplogroup D is most common in the Yupik and Chukchi, two modern indigenous groups in northeast Siberia whose ancestors are thought to have played a significant role in the peopling of the Americas.

This information doesn't make me feel distinct in any way. It does the opposite of defining me. It only allows a closer picture of how much movement I am made of. My eyes share the epicanthic folds of people from many parts of the world — a biologising of my body to classify it among others. But biology is insufficient when it comes to belonging. The DNA that forms me — the east, west, north and south of me — is no more meaningful to my sense of belonging than the stories my mother told me as a child or the stories I told myself of coming from everywhere. I *do* come from everywhere. But the books that have fed and ignited my imagination are far more defining than my DNA. A test of this type can only tell us about how human beings adapt to their surroundings on the planet, how we change, how we are infected by one another, and how we evolve features to help us to survive. Whereas books, literature, art: these show us all the possibilities of living itself.

Someone once said that race is like six o'clock.[2] That specific hour doesn't actually exist, but we agree upon it as a fixed point in the day, a social idea. Both real and a construction. To deal with the idea is easy: I can dismiss it, demonstrate its absurdity by invoking the speed of light and the deja vus and time warps of my own experience. Just like six o'clock, the biological make-up of a human being is not a prescription for how to perceive that being. Time is mysterious and we've all experienced its tricks. We don't have to agree that a day is divided into hours, but most of us go along with it. To deal with the real aspect of six o'clock (to have to make appointments and not miss flights) and the real aspect of race (to ask myself who I am in the face of pointed, perpetual anti-black violence and discrimination) is a different kind of challenge altogether.

I spent most of my early life feeling I didn't belong anywhere, which paralysed me, personally and politically. That feeling was a product of the plantation. It served to divide me from myself and from others with whom I belong in action, in resistance. The shame of living in the master's house is debilitating, but my lack of belonging has been a red herring. I don't want to belong anywhere on the plantation. I have lacked the revolutionary leadership to be

Quamina, the enslaved man leading a rebellion, and I have been the obedient 'other'.

But it's time for disobedience. For action. *Oh, the world*. In our dispossession and our rage, we need to ask different questions. The single most powerful tool we have is our language and its ability to reinvent realities. We can talk and listen, undergo a collective psychoanalysis that sees us uncovering all that is difficult to know: the sources of shame and how we might move on from them.

I desire a new language of belonging. A *who-are-you* space to gather in with others, rather than the biological 'what'am I. This new language finds the political in the personal, and it requires me to ask who I am in the face of any new race-making that might be taking place. Who in me is the slave, who the plantation owner, who the indentured labourer, the bounty keeper, who the collaborator, who the perpetrator, who the victim? Who am I othering as I write, as I speak, as I travel, as I shop? What borders am I erecting, who am I when I don't feel I have enough?

My mother calls me, late, not remembering the five-hour gap between us. But she is lively on the phone, not anxious, her memory sharp, and it seems like she is in control of the week's events, telling me she's going back to the cottage in a few days. I suspect she has her calendar in front of her as we speak, but I give her the benefit of the doubt as she jokes about the raccoons she's having a battle with in her garden and how they keep her busy inventing new ways to keep them out of her rubbish bins. She also asks me if I've seen various news items from CNN, which she watches constantly throughout the day and which causes her to call me in alarm if there are any 'events' in London. I remind her that I don't watch CNN, but I ask if she's seen that a rich man is talking about colonising Mars and taking all the other rich people with him. Either there or to New Zealand, I add.

'Good, let them go!' she says, with a giggle.

I tell her that in my daily news feed I saw an article detailing the fact that the richest people in the UK have increased their wealth by 183 per cent in ten years, while more and more London workers are queuing up for foodbanks and handouts, because with the rising cost of living they have to choose between rent and food. She goes quiet, and then changes the subject: this one hurts. I don't mention another story I've read recently, from Fisheries and Oceans Canada, which spotted and tracked a twenty-year-old mother orca whale — an endangered species — carrying her dead new-born calf through the waters of the Pacific Ocean, in the Strait of Juan de Fuca off Vancouver Island. The mother balanced the still-born calf on her forehead or pushed it to the surface as she swam with it, for day upon day, never allowing it to sink, keeping it afloat on her own body. While it is not unusual for cetaceans to mourn their young, this particular demonstration of grief lasted at least seventeen days — the longest ever documented. The mother finally let the calf go. The Centre for Whale Research claimed that once her tour of grief was over, her behaviour became 'remarkably frisky'.[3] I imagine this orca like my mother: playful, surviving, but still marked by grief.

After other small exchanges, out of the blue, she says, 'What's going to become of the world?' I get my tendency for dramatic and impossible questions from her. I tell her that I have hope. I don't excuse the fact that hope can be blind or that hope alone will never dismantle hierarchical human relationships or the plundering human spirit, because part of me has always tried to protect her.

In public conversations and actions around race, politics, ecology we can't leave out emotions — like grief, sadness, anger, shame — because these are key to action. We can't explore and achieve equality without them. Depression and inertia, which seem to flourish everywhere I look these days, are, according to most psychotherapists, the outcome of repressed anger. I am angry at inequality. Like my desire for a new language of belonging, I desire a new language of politics, social justice, struggle, rebellion. Revolution.

While we make changes that will take into account the physical and material needs of all people, I want to include our emotional health, our mental health — the fragility of what it means to be alive. I want to stop being embarrassed, when it comes to politics, by my use of the word love. Or indeed by hate, by anger, grief, pain.

My original question — What am I? — is irrelevant. Apparently, I am a symphony. The more pertinent and on-going question is *Who* am I? It's a perennial and evolving investigation into what kind of person I am, what change I want to effect and whether my actions hurt other people. I need to remain vigilant, to keep an eye on history at all moments, to read and read and read and never pretend that I fully know the answer to anything at all except what my own responsibility requires. And in turn to demand of others that they know how to answer the question too.

Who *are* you?

I fold my arms on the desk, put my head onto them and rest here. I don't disappear. I wait.

Notes

What Are You?

Epigraph from McCloskey, Robert (1961), *Make Way for Ducklings*. New York: The Viking Press.

1   Quoted in Curran, Andrew S. (2011), *The Anatomy of Blackness: science and slavery in an age of enlightenment*. Baltimore: Johns Hopkins University Press.

2   Smedley, Audrey (1997), 'Origin of The Idea of Race', *Anthropology Newsletter*. http://www.pbs.org/race/000_About/002_04-background-02–09.htm [accessed Feb 23, 2018]

Chapter 1: Nose

Epigraph from Ellison, Ralph (2001), *Invisible Man*. New York: Penguin Classics.

Chapter 2: Lips

Epigraph from Rhys, Jean (1966), *Wide Sargasso Sea*. London: Andre Deutsch.

Chapter 3: Eyes

Epigraph from Choy, Wayson (1995), *The Jade Peony*. Vancouver: Douglas McIntyre.

1   Aide memoire, 'Increasing Immigration to Canada', n.d. National Archives of Canada, RG 76, vol. 816, File 551-10-1963, pt. 2. See also 'Draft Immigration Program — 1963–1964', National Archives of Canada, RG 76, vol. 816, File 551-10-1963, pt. 1.

2   Quoted in Eze, Emmanuel Chukwudi, 'The Colour of Reason: The Idea of "Race" in Kant's Anthropology' in Eze (ed.) (1997), *Postcolonial African Philosophy: a critical reader*. Cambridge MA: Blackwell.

Chapter 4: Hair

Epigraph from Morrison, Toni (1999), *The Bluest Eye*. New York: Vintage.

Chapter 5: Ass

Epigraph from Shange, Ntozake (1997), *for colored girls who have considered suicide / when the rainbow is enuf*. New York: Macmillan Press.

1   Thanks to Christina Sharpe for opening up a vista to see how images and their replication over time, even in attempts to redeem them, can be serving the same masters of oppression that made them. See Sharpe, Christina (2010), *Monstrous Intimacies: making post-slavery subjects*. Durham and London: Duke University Press.

2   Chaudhuri, Nupur (1994), 'Memsahibs and their Servants in Nineteenth-century India', *Women's History Review*, Volume 3, Number 4.

Chapter 6: Bones

Epigraph from Highway, Tomson (1998), *Kiss of the Fur Queen*. Toronto: Doubleday Canada.

1   Walcott, Derek (2007), 'The Sea is History', *Selected Poems*. New York: Farrar, Straus and Giroux.

Chapter 7: Skin

Epigraph from Roy, Arundhati (1997), *The God of Small Things*. London: Flamingo.

1   See Herring, Cedric, Keith, Verna M., and Horton, Hayward Derrick (eds) (2003), *Skin Deep: how race and complexion matter in the 'color blind' era*. Chicago: University of Illinois Press.

2   Model Irene Major, quoted in Ley, Rebecca, 'As Holland & Barrett come under fire for selling a controversial skin lightening cream … The women who'll do anything to have whiter skin', *Daily Mail*, 24 November 2014. http://www.dailymail.co.uk/femail/article-2850927/As-Holland-Barrett-come-fire-selling-controversial-skin-lightening-cream-women-wholl-whiter-skin.html

3   Abdul Latif Mohamed (2003), *Genocide in Rwanda: The Interplay of Human Capital, Scarce Resources and Social Cohesion*. Submitted

in partial fulfillment of the requirements for the degree of Master of Arts in Security Studies, Naval Postgraduate School, California, December 2003.

Chapter 8: Blood

Epigraph from Phillips, Caryl (1995), *Crossing the River*. New York: Vintage Books.

1   National Human Genome Research Institute, https://www.genome. gov/12011238/an-overview-of-the-human-genome-project/

2   Beckford, W. (1790), *A Descriptive Account of the Island of Jamaica with Remarks upon the Cultivation of the Sugar-Cane, throughout the different Seasons of the Year, and chiefly considered a Picturesque Point of View; Also Observations and Reflections upon what would probably be the Consequences of an Abolition of the Slave-Trade, and the Emancipation of the Slaves*. London: Printed for T. and J. Egerton, Whitehall.

Double Helix

Epigraph from Carson, Anne (1998), 'The Glass Essay' in *Glass, Irony and God*. London: Jonathan Cape.

1   Keys, David, 'Details of horrific first voyages in transatlantic slave trade revealed', *The Independent*, 17 August 2018. https://www. independent.co.uk/news/world/americas/transatlantic-slave-trade-voyages-ships-log-details-africa-america-atlantic-ocean-deaths-disease-a8494546.html?amp&ocid=St&__twitter_impression=true

2   Attributed to Bagate, Maïmouna F. in Fields, Karen E. and Fields, Barbara J. (2012), *Racecraft: the soul of inequality in American life*. New York: Verso.

3   Xu, Xiao, 'Orca whale 'Tahlequah' releases dead calf after longest documented mourning period', *The Globe and Mail*, 12 August 2018. https://www.theglobeandmail.com/canada/british-columbia/article-orca-whale-tahlequah-releases-dead-calf-after-longest-documented/

Selected References

Alston, D. (2015), 'A Forgotten Diaspora: The Children of Enslaved and "Free Coloured" Women and Highland Scots in Guyana Before Emancipation', *Northern Scotland*, 6(1), pp. 49-69.

Alston, D. (n.d.) *Slaves and Highlanders | Home*. Spanglefish.com. Available at: http://www.spanglefish.com/SlavesandHighlanders/. (accessed 6 February 2019).

Anolik, R. and Howard, D. (2004), *The Gothic Other: Racial and Social Constructions in the Literary Imagination*. Jefferson: McFarland & Co.

Bailyn, B. and Morgan, P. (1991) *Strangers Within the Realm: Cultural Margins of the First British Empire*. Chapel Hill: The University of North Carolina Press.

Baldwin, J. and Peck, R. (2017), *I Am Not Your Negro*. New York and London: Penguin Classics.

Beckford, W. (1790), *A Descriptive Account of the Island of Jamaica with Remarks upon the Cultivation of the Sugar-Cane, throughout the different Seasons of the Year, and chiefly considered a Picturesque Point of View; Also Observations and Reflections upon what would probably be the Consequences of an Abolition of the Slave-Trade, and the Emancipation of the Slaves*. London: Printed for T. and J. Egerton, Whitehall.

Bergner, G. (1995), 'Who Is That Masked Woman? Or, the Role of Gender in Fanon's Black Skin, White Masks', *PMLA*, 110(1), pp.75-88. DOI: 10.2307/463196 (Accessed 19 January 2019).

Bernasconi, R. and Dotson, K. (2005), *Race, Hybridity, and Miscegenation Vol. 1-3*. Bristol, England: Thoemmes Continuum.

Bolland, O. (1996), 'Indentured Labor, Caribbean Sugar: Chinese and Indian Migrants to the British West Indies, 1838-1918, by Walton Look Lai', *International Labor and Working-class History*, 49, pp. 217-219.

British Library. (n.d.) *Oracle bones were used for divination over three thousand years ago in ancient China and they are the oldest items held in the British Library*. Available at: https://www.bl.uk/collection-items/chinese-oracle-bone (accessed 6 February 2019).

Burke, L. ed. (1848), *Ethnological Journal: a Magazine of Ethnography, Phrenology, and Archæology, Considered as Elements of the Science of Races, with the Applications of this Science to Education, Legislation and Social Progress*. London: General Reference Collection, no. 1 June

1848 - no. 10 Mar. 1849, then n.s. (without "Phrenology" in the title)
no. 1 Jan. 1845.

Carroll, A. (2003), *Dark Smiles: Race and Desire in George Eliot*.
Athens, Ohio: University of Ohio Press.

Chatterjee, P. (2000), 'De/Colonizing the Exotic: Teaching "Asian
Women" in a U.S. Classroom', *Frontiers: A Journal of Women Studies*,
21(1/2), pp. 87-110.

Clark, W. (1823), *Ten Views of the Island of Antigua in which
are represented the process of sugar making, and the employment of the
Negroes, in the field, boiling-house and distillery / from the drawings
made by William Clark*. London: Thomas Clay, Ludgate-Hill.

Cho, L. (2002), 'Rereading Chinese Head Tax Racism: Redress,
Stereotype, and Antiracist Critical Practice', *Essays on Canadian
Writing*, 75, pp. 62-84.

Coates, T. (2018), *I'm Not Black, I'm Kanye*. The Atlantic. Available at:
https://www.theatlantic.com/entertainment/archive/2018/05/im-not-
black-im-kanye/559763/ (accessed 6 February 2019).

Collini, S. (1977), 'Liberalism and the Legacy of Mill',
The Historical Journal, 20(1), pp.237-254.

Coleman, Daniel and Goellnicht, D., ed. (2002), *Essays on Canadian
Writing*, 75. Montreal: ECW Press.

Comins, D. W. D. (1893), *Note on Emigration from the East Indies to St Lucia*. Calcutta: Bengal Secretariat Press. Held by British Library: Asian and African Studies.

Craton, M. (1991), 'Reluctant Creoles: The Planters' World in the British West Indies', in Bailyn, B. and Morgan, P. (2012), *Strangers Within the Realm: Cultural Margins of the First British Empire*. Chapel Hill: The University of North Carolina Press.

Crawford, M. (1989), *Scenes from the History of The Chinese in Guyana*. Georgetown, Guyana: Marlene Kwok Crawford.

Crawford, M. (2008), *Dilution Anxiety and the Black Phallus*. Columbus, Ohio: The Ohio State University Press.

Curran, A. (2011), *The Anatomy of Blackness: Science and Slavery in an Age of Enlightenment*. Baltimore: Johns Hopkins University Press.

Das, D. and Morrow, C., ed. (2018), *Unveiling Desire: Fallen Women in Literature, Culture and Films of the East*. New Brunswick: Rutgers University Press.

Delany, S. (2005) *About Writing: Seven Essays, Four Letters and Five Interviews*. Middletown: Wesleyan University Press.

Douglass, F. (1892), *Life and Times of Frederick Douglass, Written by Himself: The Illustrated Edition*. Boston: De Wolfe & Fiske Co.

Drummond, L. (1974), *The Outskirts of the Earth: A Study of Amerindian Ethnicity on the Pomeroon River, Guyana*. PhD. Chicago University.

Eze, E., ed. (1997), *Postcolonial African Philosophy: A Critical Reader*. Cambridge: Blackwell Publishers.

Fairmann, J. (1859), *Cheap Sugar; or, Coolie Immigration to the West Indies. In a series of letters reprinted from 'The Witness'*. Edinburgh: Paton and Ritchie.

Fields, B. and Fields, K. (2014) *Racecraft: The Soul of Inequality in American Life*. London and New York: Verso Books.

Gent, R. (1657), *A True & Exact History of the Island of Barbados: Illustrated with a Mapp of the Island, as also the Principall Trees and Plants there, set forth in their due Proportions and Shapes, drawne out by their severall and respective Scales: Together with the Ingenio that makes the sugar, with the Plots of severall Houses, Roomes, and other places, that are used in the whole processe of Sugar-making viz. the Grinding-room, the Boyling-room, the Filling-room, the Curing-house, Still-house, and Furnace; all cut in copper*. London: Printed for Humphrey Mosely at the Prince's Armes in St. Paul's Churchyard.

Glenn, E. (2009), *Shades of Difference: Why Skin Color Matters*. Stanford: Stanford University Press.

Grainger, J. (1764), *The Sugar Cane: A Poem in Four Books*. London: R. and J. Dodsley.

Gwyn, J. (1998), *Excessive Expectations: Maritime Commerce and the Economic Development of Nova Scotia, 1740-1870*. Montreal: McGill-Queen's University Press.

Haider, A. (2018), *Mistaken Identity: Race and Class in the Age of Trump*. New York: Verso Books.

Hall, D. (1989), *In Miserable Slavery: Thomas Thistlewood in Jamaica, 1750-86*. London and Basingstoke: Macmillan Press.

Hamilton, C. (2008), '"Am I Not a Man and a Brother?" Phrenology and Anti-slavery', *Slavery & Abolition*, 29(2), pp.173-187.

Hares, L. (1960), *The History of Sugar*. Georgetown, Guyana: British Guiana Sugar Producers' Association.

Huub, E. (2013), 'Unknown Father in Suriname, 1838 to 1873', *Historical Methods*, 46(4), pp. 203-219.

Iyengar, S. (2005), *Shades of Difference: Mythologies of Skin Color in Early Modern England*. Philadelphia: University of Pennsylvania Press.

Jackson, J., Brown, T., Williams, D., Torres, M., Sellers S., and Brown, K. (1996), 'Racism and the Physical and Mental Health Status of African Americans: A Thirteen Year Panel Study', *Ethn Dis*, 6(1-2), pp. 132-147.

Jahoda, G. (2009), 'Intra-European Racism in Nineteenth-Century Anthropology', *History and Anthropology*, 20(1), pp. 37-56.

James, C. (1989), *The Black Jacobins: Toussaint L'ouverture and the San Domingo Revolution.* 2nd ed. New York: Vintage Books.

Jenkins, E. (1871), *The Coolie: His Rights and Wrongs.* Reprint, Georgetown, Guyana: The Caribbean Press for the Government of Guyana, 2010.

Jones, S. (1997), *In the Blood: Gods, Genes and Destiny.* London: Flamingo.

Joshi, R. (1997), 'Genocide in Rwanda: The Root Causes', *East African Journal of Peace and Human Rights*, 3(1), pp. 51-91.

Kant, I. (1978), *Anthropology from a Pragmatic Point of View,* translated by Victor Lyle Dowdell, p. 6n. Carbondale: Southern Illinois University Press.

Kendi, I. (2016), *Stamped From the Beginning: The Definitive History of Racist Ideas in America.* New York: National Books.

Lam, S.-c. (1990), *War and Imperialism: The Origins of the Sino-Japanese War of 1894.* Hong Kong: History Critique Publication Studio.

Laurence, K. (1995), 'Crowns of Glory, Tears of Blood: The Demerara Slave Rebellion of 1823 by Emilia Viotti da Costa', *Labor History,* 36(4), pp. 664-665.

Laurence, K. (1980), *The Development of Medical Services in British Guiana and Trinidad, 1841-1873; The evolution of Long-term Labour Contracts in*

Trinidad and British Guiana, 1834-1863. Mona, Jamaica: Department of History, University of the West Indies.

Laurence, K. (1971), *Immigration into the West Indies in the 19 th Century*. St. Lawrence, Barbados: Caribbean Universities Press.

Laurence, K. (1994), *A Question of Labour: Indentured Immigration into Trinidad and British Guiana, 1875-1917*. Kingston, Jamaica: Ian Randle; London: James Currey.

Lean, J. (2002), *The Secret Lives of Slaves: Berbice, 1819 to 1827*. PhD. University of Canterbury.

Ligon, R. (n.d.) *A True and Exact History of the Island of Barbados*. Kingston, Jamaica: University College of the West Indies.

Look Lai, W., ed. (2006), *Essays on the Chinese Diaspora in the Caribbean*. St. Augustine, Trinidad: University of the West Indies.

Losurdo, D. (2011), *Liberalism: A Counter-History*. London: Verso Books.

Mali, J. (2015), 'The Making of Modern Liberalism', *The European Legacy*, 21(1), pp. 107-109.

Mann, J. (2016), *The Search for a New National Identity: The Rise of Multiculturalism in Canada and Australia, 1890s-1970s*. New York: Peter Lang Publishing.

Mellinkoff, R. (1994), *Outcasts: Signs of Otherness in Northern European Art of the Late Middle Ages Vol. 1-2*. Berkeley: University of California Press.

Menezes, M. (1983), *Amerindian Life in Guyana*. Georgetown, Guyana: Ministry of Education, Social Development and Culture.

Menezes, M. (1979), *The Amerindians in Guyana, 1803-73*. London: Frank Cass.

Mies, M. with a foreword by Federici, S. (2014), *Patriarchy and Accumulation on a World Scale*. London: Zed Books.

Mintz, S. (1985), *Sweetness and Power: The Place of Sugar in Modern History*. Kindle Reprint, New York: Penguin Books, 1986.

Moore, B. (1987), *Race, Power and Social Segmentation in Colonial Society: Guyana After Slavery, 1838-1891*. New York: Gordon and Breach Science Publishers.

Neighbors, H. and Williams, D. (2001), 'Heath Issues in the Black Community', in Braithwaite, R. and Taylor, S., eds. *Heath in the Black Community*. San Francisco: Jossey-Bass Publishers. pp. 99-128.

NPR Radio Podcast (2017), *Brazil in Black and White*. Rough Translation.

Omnium J. and Higgins M. (1848), *Is Cheap Sugar the Triumph of Free Trade? A Second Letter To the Rt. Hon. Lord John Russell*. London: James Ridgway, Piccadilly.

Patel, R. and Moore, J. (2018), *A History of the World in Seven Cheap Things*. London: Verso Books.

Peakman, J. (2009), *Sexual Perversions, 1670-1890*. London: Palgrave Macmillan.

Piper, A. (1992), 'Passing for White, Passing for Black', *Transition*, 58, pp. 4-32.

Prasso, S. (2005), *The Asian Mystique: Dragon Ladies, Geisha Girls & Our Fantasies of the Exotic Orient*. New York: Public Affairs.

Prince, A. (2010), *The Politics of Black Women's Hair*. London, Ontario: Insomniac Press.

Rediker, M. (2007), *The Slave Ship*. New York: Viking.

Report on The Condition of Indian Immigrants in the Four British Colonies: Trinidad, British Guiana or Demerara, Jamaica and Fiji and the Dutch Colony of Surinam or Dutch Guiana. (1914) Simla: Government Central Press.

Riland, J. (1827), *Memoirs of a West India Planter*. London: Hamilton Adams & Co.

Ritchie, J. (1844), *Thoughts on Slavery and Cheap Sugar; A letter to the Members and Friends of the British and Foreign Anti-Slavery Society*. London.

Roberts, D. (1993), 'Racism and Patriarchy in the Meaning of

Motherhood', *Faculty Scholarship at Penn Law*, 595.

Rodney, W. (1979), *Guyanese Sugar Plantations in the Late Nineteenth Century: A Contemporary Description from the 'Argosy'*. Georgetown, Guyana: Release Publishers.

Ryan, A. (2012), *The Making of Modern Liberalism*. Princeton: Princeton University Press.

Seecharan, C. (1999), *Bechu: "Bound Coolie" Radical in British Guiana 1894-1901*. Kingston, Jamaica: University of West Indies Press.

Seecharan, C. (2005), *Sweetening Bitter Sugar: Jock Campbell, the Booker Reformer in British Guiana 1934-1966*. Kingston, Jamaica: Ian Randle Publishers.

Sharpe, C. (2016), *In the Wake: On Blackness and Being*. Durham: Duke University Press.

Sharpe, C. (2010), *Monstrous Intimacies: Making Post-Slavery Subjects*. Durham: Duke University Press.

Stanley, T. (2011), *Contesting White Supremacy: School Segregation, Anti-Racism, and the Making of Chinese Canadians*. Vancouver: University of British Columbia Press.

Staum, M. (2003), *Labeling People: French Scholars on Society, Face, and Empire, 1815-1848*. Montreal: McGill-Queen's University Press.

Stiffler, D. (1982), *Music of the coastal Amerindians of Guyana: The Arawak, Carib & Warrau* [CD]. Guyana: Folkways Records.

Sue-A-Quan, T. (2003), *Cane Ripples: the Chinese in Guyana*. Vancouver: Cane Press.

Sue-A-Quan, T. (1999), *Cane Reapers: Chinese Indentured Immigrants in Guyana*. Vancouver: Riftswood Publishing.

Susman, R. (2014), *The Myth of Race: The Troubling Persistence of an Unscientific Idea*. Cambridge: Harvard University Press.

Sweetmeats, L. o. (1841), *To the working classes. Cheap sugar calculation. The tax on free labour sugar is 24 shillings a hundred weight, and dry blown West India sugar sells in this country at an average of 60s. 6d. for 112lbs ... All that the working man can save, therefore is little more than a half of a farthing on one pound of sugar. This is called cheap sugar! What a farce!!* [Poster]. Printed by Pyrke, Deptford Bridge, Deptford. 24 June. 36cm. x 24cm.

Taylor, C. (2019), 'Education Is the Key to Prosperity: The Barbadian Education System and 20th-Century Black Barbadian Migrants in Canada', *Sage Journals*, 45(5), pp. 453-473.

Triadafilopoulos, T. (2013), 'Chapter Two: Dismantling White Canada: Race, Rights and the Origins of the Points System', in Triadafilopoulos, T. (ed.) *Wanted and Welcome? Policies for Highly Skilled Immigrants in Comparative Perspective*. New York: Springer, pp. 15-37.

Võ, L. and Sciachitano, M. (2000), 'Moving Beyond "Exotics, Whores, and Nimble Fingers": Asian American Women in a New Era of Globalization and Resistance', *Frontiers: A Journal of Women Studies*, XXI(1/2), pp. 1-19.

Walvin, J. (2017), *Sugar: The World Corrupted, from Slavery to Obesity*. London: Hachette UK.

Wilberforce, S. (1848), *Cheap Sugar Means Cheap Slaves. Speech in the House of Lords, Feb. 7, 1848, against the admission of slave labour sugar on equal terms with free labour produce. With an appendix illustrative of the impetus given to the slave trade by the Bill of 1846.* 2nd ed. London.

William L. Clements Library. (n.d.) *Sugar in the Atlantic World | Case 6 Sugar and Slavery*. Available at: http://clements.umich.edu/exhibits/online/sugarexhibit/sugar06.php (Accessed 6 February 2019).

Willis, A. (1882), *A Treatise on Human Nature and Physiognomy*. Chicago: Cameron, Amberg & Co.

Wilson, L., Wilson, C. and Johnson, B. (2010), 'Race and Health in Guyana: An Empirical Assessment from Survey Data', *Caribbean Studies*, 38(1), pp. 37-58.

Wolfthal, D. (1994), 'Outcasts: Signs of Otherness in Northern European Art of the Late Middle Ages. (California Studies in the History of Art 32.). Vol. 1, Vol. 2 by Ruth Mellinkoff', *Studies in Iconography*, 16, pp. 243-246.

Acknowledgements

Bodies and spirits. I reach back through time to thank them: the ancestors, my grandmother and other grandparents, my father. In the present, I owe this book to those without whom I am invisible: my mother, my sister, my brother, my nieces and nephews, my cousins in London, Canada and Guyana. Particular thanks to Sean McWatt for anecdotes and his knowledge of anatomy, and to Wayne McWatt for his boundless memory and invaluable archival material.

Thank you to Felicity Nichols for leading me through the shadows.

This book exists as a result of the support of the Eccles British Library Writer's Award, and I was honoured to have the help of the staff at the Eccles Centre at the British Library, particularly Jean Petrovic, Elizabeth Cooper, Cara Rodway and Philip Hatfield.

Philip Gwyn Jones pointed me towards the award, and he, along with Anne Collins, supported the project even before it was written. They also challenged me: Philip demanding that I should be bold, and Anne, with her meticulous, uncompromising edit, encouraging me never to hide behind my ideas.

I am deeply grateful to many others whose generosity and engagement contributed to this book:

The early readers and interlocutors who helped me find courage and voice: Stephanie Young, Marko Jobst, Fides Krucker, Ian Rashid, Peter Ride, Stephen Maddison and Tim Atkins.

China Miéville and Rosie Warren for breakfasts, comradery and critical feedback.

Christina Sharpe for her sensitive, insightful critique, which opened up new vistas.

Molly Slight, my editor at Scribe, who has been a steady champion and companion throughout the journey, diligently and carefully bringing this book into the world.

The teams at Scribe, Random House Canada, and Penguin Random House Canada.

My colleagues at the University of East Anglia who read some or all of the manuscript and supported me in my rookie year with them: Alison Donnell, Anshuman Mondal, Rebecca Stott, Claire Hynes, Tiffany Atkinson, Petra Rau, Naomi Wood.

Senica Maltese for her careful work on references.

Andrew Kidd.

Meg Wheeler and everyone at Westwood Creative whose support has helped me through moments of distinctly Transatlantic anxiety.

Finally, I don't have the right words to express my gratitude to my dear friend and literary agent, Jackie Kaiser, whose guidance, encouragement, remedies to tackle fatigue, along with invaluable abstract conversations about the unseen and unknowable, have been indispensable for many years.